EQUAL OPPORTUNITIES COMMISSION

Separate Tables?
An investigation into single-sex setting in mathematics

Stuart Smith

LONDON HER MAJESTY'S STATIONERY OFFICE

Crown copyright 1986
First published 1986

ISBN 0 11 701292 0

The research on which this report is based
was supported by the Equal Opportunities
Commission. The views expressed are those
of the author and do not necessarily
represent the views of the Commission.

Equal Opportunities Commission
Overseas House, Quay Street,
Manchester M3 3HN

Also in London, Cardiff and Glasgow.

Acknowledgements

I am grateful to the Equal Opportunities Commission for the funding which enabled me to undertake this investigation, and I should like to thank all those officers of EOC, and most particularly Ron Barrowclough and Karen Clarke, who have consistently given me their advice and support.

I am most indebted to Dr. Stuart Trickey of Sheffield City Polytechnic for the time he has devoted to reading this report, and for the many helpful suggestions he has made to improve its content.

Gordon Taylor, retired Head of Maths at Stamford High School designed many items on the four short tests. I greatly appreciated this assistance and his ready advice and support. I should also like to thank Mr. Derek Foxman of the National Foundation for Educational Research for providing copies of the APU Mathematics Attitude Questionnaire at extremely short notice. The use of several APU items in the four short tests is acknowledged.

My daughter Nancy spent many days checking the marking of the tests and other calculations associated with this investigation. Her assistance was much appreciated. I should also like to thank the Tameside Education Committee for the use of various premises at Stamford High School.

Finally, I could not have attempted this research without the full support of Peter Beetlestone, Headmaster of Stamford High School, and his teaching staff. Many visits were made to the school, and I was always received with courtesy. I am deeply grateful to the many teachers and pupils who willingly gave their time to this investigation.

Stuart Smith

Contents

	Page
Summary	1
1. Background and objectives	4
2. Design of the study	9
3. A third year test of numeracy	12
4. Maths performance in the fourth year	17
5. Pupils' attitudes towards Maths	21
6. External examination results	26
7. Girls who find Maths difficult	30
8. The teachers' views	36
9. Conclusions	40

APPENDICES

I	The organisation of Maths at Stamford High School	44
II	Statistical methods and significance tests	46
III	NFER Non-verbal test DH: Analysis	48
IV	Tameside Numerary Test: Analysis	49
V	Four short tests: Analysis	51
VI	APU Maths Attitude Questionnaire: Analysis	52

References 55

Tables

		Page
Table 2.1	NFER test DH scores: all pupils	10
Table 2.2	A sample of DH scores produced by the matching process	11
Table 3.1	Tameside numeracy test: relative difficulty of topics	13
Table 4.1	Four short tests: mean scores, by group	17
Table 5.1	Difficulty statements in which the difference between the responses of boys and girls was significant	22
Table 5.2	Utility statements in which there were significant differences between segregated girls and other groups of pupils	23
Table 5.3	Enjoyment statement in which there was a significant difference between the responses of segregated boys and segregated girls	24
Table 6.1	Maths external examination results: Detailed breakdown	26
Table 6.2	Maths external examination results: Simplified breakdown	27
Table 9.1	GCE 'O' level passes in Maths, by sex	40

Figures

Figure 3.1	Tameside numeracy test: item by item comparisons of performance	14
Figure 4.1	Four short tests: item by item comparisons of performance	18
Figure 6.1	External examination results: analysis by paired pupils	28

Summary

1. Background and objectives

1.1 In recent times, the Mathematics education of girls has attracted a great deal of attention. Much of this attention has concentrated on the comparative achievements of boys and girls, and careful consideration has also been given to the question of whether boys and girls are likely to be more successful in Maths when taught in single sex or co-educational classes.

1.2 This investigation compares a group of boys and a group of girls who were taught Maths in segregated sets for five years with groups of boys and girls who were taught in conventional mixed sets for the same period.

1.3 All the pupils involved in this investigation attended Stamford High School in Tameside from the age of 11 to 16. This school has taken a keen interest for many years in the under-achievement of girls in Maths.

2. Design of the study

2. The four groups of pupils involved in this investigation (referred to as mixed boys, mixed girls, segregated boys and segregated girls) were matched by ability on a non-verbal reasoning test taken in the first term of the first year.

3. A third year test of numeracy

3.1 In the Tameside Numeracy Test (taken by the pupils in the second term of the third year) the segregated girls performed significantly better than the mixed girls on six of the 13 topics tested. This suggested that as far as the basic numerical skills covered by this test were concerned, the segregated girls had gained some benefit from single sex setting.

3.2 There was little difference between the performance of the two groups of boys.

3.3 There was also little difference between the overall performance of the mixed boys and mixed girls and between that of the segregated boys and segregated girls. When the most difficult items of the test were analysed separately, however, it was found that the performance of both groups of boys was significantly better than that of the two groups of girls they were paired with.

4. Maths performance in the fourth year

4.1 Towards the end of the fourth year, the pupils attempted four short tests which had been designed to supplement the Tameside Numeracy Test. These short tests contained many items requiring problem-solving skills.

4.2 The overall results achieved by the two groups of boys were very similar as were the results achieved by the two groups of girls. This suggested that as far as the work covered by these tests was concerned, segregated setting had had little effect on either boys or girls.

4.3 The overall performance of both groups of boys on these tests however was significantly better than that of the two groups of girls they were paired with. These differences were greatest on the tests dealing with Geometry and Mensuration and this was true whether the pupils had been taught in mixed or segregated sets.

5. Pupils' attitudes towards Maths

5.1 The pupils also completed the Assessment of Performance Unit (APU) Mathematics Attitude Questionnaire at the end of the fourth year. This questionnaire measured the attitude of pupils to Maths on separate difficulty, utility and enjoyment scales.

5.2 There was no significant difference in the responses of the two groups of boys to all three of these scales which suggested that segregated setting had had little effect on the attitudes of boys to Maths.

5.3 Mixed girls perceived Maths as being significantly more useful than segregated girls, but there was little difference in the responses of the two groups of girls to the other two attitude scales.

5.4 Both groups of girls perceived Maths as a much more difficult subject than the two groups of boys. Additionally, segregated boys considered Maths to be significantly more useful and more enjoyable than segregated girls.

5.5 When the scores of individual girls on both the short tests and the attitude scales were compared with the scores of the boys they were paired with, generally speaking the differences were greater between average and above average ability boys and girls than between below average ability boys and girls. This was true whether the pupils had been taught in segregated sets or not.

6. External Examination Results

6.1 In the GCE 'O' level and CSE Maths exminations, the performance of the two groups of boys was very similar, and the same was true of the two groups of girls. These results suggested that segregated setting had had little effect on the overall performance of either boys or girls in external Maths examinations.

6.2 Both groups of boys performed better in these examinations than the two groups of girls, although the differences were not statistically significant.

7. Girls who find Maths difficult

7.1 Interviews were conducted with a number of fifth year girls who perceived Maths as a difficult subject.

7.2 The majority of these girls believed that their difficulties with Maths began sometime between the start of the second year and the beginning of exam courses in the fourth year.

7.3 Girls who had been taught in mixed sets were generally critical of the behaviour of the boys in Maths lessons, and this behaviour probably did have an adverse effect on some of the girls. Nevertheless, the girls mainly attributed their difficulties in Maths to the speed with which they were expected to move from topic to topic.

7.4 These girls generally worked in pairs or small groups and there was virtually no positive contact with boys.

7.5 Most of the girls who had been taught Maths in segregated sets approved of this arrangement, but a minority suggested that mixed sets would have been livelier and more competitive.

7.6 Maths teachers were highly regarded by the girls of both groups. Assistance from the Maths teachers was said to be readily available.

8. The teachers' views

8.1 Six full-time Maths teachers were also interviewed. All of them expressed mixed feelings about single sex setting, although the initial reservations which some of them had felt towards segregation had largely disappeared.

8.2 They all believed that in general girls gained more from segregated setting than boys, and that it was more beneficial for younger pupils than older ones.

8.3 The majority of these teachers believed that segregated setting created discipline problems with the older pupils (particularly boys). Another disadvantage was that segregation inhibited fine setting and this handicapped the more able boys and girls in particular.

9. Conclusions

9.1 In recent years, there has been a remarkable improvement in the number of girls from the school who have been successful in the 'O' Level Maths examination. This improvement (achieved both by girls taught in mixed sets and girls taught in segregated sets alike) appears to be closely related to a number of steps which have been taken to end the masculine image of Maths in school.

9.2 The results of this investigation suggest that a great deal can be done to improve the performance of girls in Maths without recourse to segregated setting. Nevertheless, it is felt that single sex sets in the first and second years could be worth encouraging particularly if a special scheme of work designed to meet the needs of girls in Maths were developed.

1 Background and objectives

Introduction

Despite some improvement in recent years, secondary schoolgirls still do not perform as well as boys in Maths examinations at age 16. Fewer girls than boys attempt 'O' level Maths, and girls have a lower success rate. More girls than boys attempt CSE Maths, but boys are more successful at Grade 1 level [1].

In an Appendix to the Cockcroft Report 'Mathematics Counts' Shuard (1982) stressed the need for research in Britain into the causes of girls' comparative under-achievement in Mathematics. In her list of suggested reasons for differences in performance between boys and girls she stated that:

> "In mixed schools, in groups in which boys and girls are following the same course, there is some evidence that boys still have more opportunity to learn than do girls. Secondary school teachers have been shown to interact more with boys than they do with girls and to give more serious consideration to boy's ideas; they also give boys more opportunities to respond to higher cognitive level questions. High-achieving girls have been found to receive significantly less attention in Mathematics classes than do high-achieving boys."

It is therefore a matter of considerable interest to discover whether the establishment of segregated sets in Maths in mixed schools can have a beneficial effect on the academic performance of girls and it is equally important to discover if boys are affected by single sex setting.

The practice of segregating pupils by sex for various subjects in mixed schools is as old as co-education itself. In the past this has been done for a variety of reasons, but it is only recently that segregated classes have been introduced as a deliberate attempt to improve the relative academic performance and attitude of either boys or girls.

Research on single sex education

Research concerned with single sex setting in mixed secondary schools is very sparse: indeed, the investigation reported here is believed to be the first detailed analysis of the effects of single sex setting in Maths. By contrast, numerous researchers and statisticians have compared academic performance in mixed and single sex schools, and no subject area has attracted more attention than Maths.

For example, Pidgeon (1976) reported the results of a series of National Foundation for Educational Research Maths tests taken by some 12,000 pupils attending all types of secondary school in 1964. The results revealed that both boys and girls from single sex schools performed better in each of the age groups tested than boys and girls from mixed schools respectively. However, these results need to be qualified. Statistics published by the Department of Education and Science for 1965 show that whereas 36% of all boys' schools and 37% of all girls' schools were in the grammar school sector, only 14% of mixed schools were grammar schools. Consequently, single sex schools

---

[1] In 1983, girls comprised 47.1% of the total 'O' Level Maths entry. 53.0% of these girls passed with Grade A, B or C compared with 61.2% of boys. Girls comprised 52.5% of the CSE Maths entry, but only 15.3% of these girls achieved a Grade 1 pass compared with 18.2% of boys. (Equal Opportunities Commission, 1985).

contained a higher proportion of more able pupils than mixed schools. Furthermore, Steedman and Fogelman (1980) demonstrated that single sex schools at this time had a marked advantage in terms of social class.

In the debate concerning mixed and single sex schools, no-one has made a greater impact than Dale who devoted his career from the late 1940s until the early 1970s to comparing the two types of school. Dale, an enthusiast of co-education, conducted surveys at many levels of the education system and his findings eventually led him to conclude (1974) that:

> "the average co-educational grammar school is a happier community for both staff and pupils than the average single-sex school; it has been equally demonstrated that this happiness is not at the expense of educational progress."

With regard to Maths, Dale's work is particularly important because he reviewed the work of other researchers in this field such as Cameron (1923), Tyson (1928), King (1966), Field (1935) and Sutherland (1961). These reviews, plus his own findings led Dale (1974) to state:

> "When we consider boys and girls together, we can say that co-education in some way or other appears to exert a beneficial influence on attainment in Mathematics, as measured by external examinations and tests at the age of 16 plus. Though this cannot be said to be proved in a scientific sense there is considerable evidence in support, especially on the boys' side, while there is none whatever for any claim that sex segregation improves attainment in Mathematics."

Dale's findings were questioned by Wood and Ferguson (1974). They pointed out that much of Dale's data were out-of-date and the value of his surveys was limited in that they dealt with grammar schools alone. Furthermore, the corrections which Dale made to adjust for social class (generally to the benefit of mixed schools), were considered dubious. Ferguson and Wood proceeded to analyse the results of 100,000 pupils taking the London Board 'O' level examinations in 1973 and they concluded that with contemporary data they were: 'unable to confirm the claim made by Mr. Dale for the superior academic results of co-educational schooling.'

In a later report, Wood (1976) analysed the responses to the London Board 'O' Level Syllabus 'C' Maths papers of 1973 and 1974 and he found that girls from single sex schools did rather better than girls from mixed schools, but he went on to suggest that the single sex schools probably contained a higher proportion of more able girls.

In research connected with the National Child Development Study (NCDS), Steedman (1980) was able to measure the progress of both boys and girls between the ages of 11 and 16 in different types of secondary schools. She found that girls in girls only grammar schools made much more progress in Maths than girls in mixed grammar schools. No such difference was noted for grammar school boys however, and in all other secondary schools, single sex education offered no consistent advantage to either girls or boys. It should be noted that the number of girls involved in the study who were being educated in mixed grammar schools would have been quite small and this naturally weakens the comparison with the girls only grammar schools.

In a later study of the external exam results of pupils involved in the NCDS, Steedman (1983) concluded that as far as Maths was concerned, there was no clear case for or against single sex schools for either boys or girls.

The 1980 Survey of Mathematical Development of 15 year olds by the Assessment of Performance Unit (1982) reported that from a survey of some 700 schools, boys and girls from single sex schools had performed better on its tests than boys and girls from mixed schools respectively. Furthermore, the differences were greater for non comprehensive secondary schools than for comprehensive schools. Once again, these results need careful interpretation for there is no doubt that in 1980, single sex schools contained a higher proportion of more able pupils than mixed schools and a higher proportion of lower ability children attended mixed schools. At this time, 75% of grammar schools were single sex compared with only 30% of secondary modern schools.

Similar care needs to be taken with a survey of the 'O' level and CSE results for 1980 of schools in the Inner London Education Authority (1982). This survey showed that both boys and girls in single sex schools did better than boys and girls from mixed schools respectively in all eight of the subjects analysed (one of which was Maths). No account was taken of their differing abilities on entry into secondary school.

To summarise, most research findings indicate that both boys and girls in single sex schools achieve greater academic success than girls in mixed schools, but it is probable that this is largely the result of the differing ability of the intakes. In Bone's exhaustive research review (1983), she concluded that:

> "The consistent lead of single-sex schools in examination results makes it easy to see how the idea became current that girls do better in single-sex schools. However, it is clear from those studies which have attempted to correct the raw results of the schools by taking into account the ability of their intakes, that if an advantage exists, it is very small."

When it came to Maths, Bone stated that:

> "Girls do not appear to achieve particularly well in Mathematics at 'O' level and CSE because their schools are single-sex."

Research objectives

The purpose of the following investigation is to assess the impact of segregating by sex a number of boys and girls in a mixed secondary school for all Maths lessons over a period of five years.

This investigation has one considerable advantage over most of the previous research reported in this chapter: by comparing groups of boys and girls who have been taught Maths in single-sex sets with boys and girls of similar ability who have been taught in mixed sets *within the same school*, most of the variables which are found when pupils of different schools are compared have been eliminated.

There are of course compensating disadvantages. By confining the investigation to one school, the number of pupils involved is very small, and this naturally limits the value of the data produced. Furthermore, what may be true of one school is not necessarily true of others. The findings of this investigation do provide useful information, but it would be wrong to assume with any certainty that similar results would be obtained if a similar setting structure were to be established in other schools.

Finally, care must be taken in applying the findings of this investigation to the debate about the relative merits of mixed and single sex schools. To attend a single sex secondary school for five years is to undergo a complete education experience and its impact on any boy or girls is likely to be much greater than the effect of attending single sex classes in a particular subject in a mixed school.

The study school

Stamford High School is a co-educational 11–16 comprehensive school situated on the outskirts of Ashton-under-Lyne, a large industrial town lying six miles to the east of Manchester. The school was created in its present form by the amalgamation of two single sex secondary modern schools in 1970. This amalgamation was a stepping stone toward the development of comprehensive education in Tameside. In the event, comprehensive re-organisation was not introduced until 1980. The school is currently seven-form entry with a population of some 1,000 pupils, approximately 15% of whom are descended from Asian immigrant families (mainly from the Indian sub-continent). The catchment area is socially very mixed, and the school recruits from a large number of feeder primary schools.

Female under-achievement in maths

In the years following amalgamation, an analysis of external examination results revealed that girls, in the main, were doing less well than boys. Girls appeared to be under-achieving across the ability range, and this under-achievement, whilst found in most subject areas, was most acute in Maths.

Although the initial Maths selection test, applied to all pupils during their first term at the school, generally revealed a similar range of performance between boys and girls, by the end of the first year, the mean test score of the boys was always higher. During the second and third years, the gap between the mean scores of boys and girls in Maths tests tended to increase and boys dominated the top 25% of the mark lists. Consequently, when the external examination sets were established at the beginning of the fourth year, it was usual for boys to out-number girls by four or five to one in the top Maths sets (which prepared for 'O' level). The small groups of girls in these sets found it difficult to cope with lessons, despite having sympathetic teachers. They tended to cluster on the fringe of the class and became reluctant to draw attention to themselves by volunteering any oral contribution. They were particularly self conscious about asking the teacher for help whenever they did not understand. Meanwhile the boys were quite content to monopolise the teacher's time and attention, and 'O' level Maths came to be regarded as a male domain. It was usual for more than 20 boys to pass 'O' level Maths each year, but rare for as many as two girls to reach this standard. In the early 1970s, the majority of the Maths teachers were male, and 'O' Level Maths sets were traditionally taught by a male teacher. In the late 1970s however, three female Maths teachers were appointed to the school and this created a more even sex balance in the department.

During this period, the Maths department held a number of meetings to discuss various means of improving the academic performance of the girls. The syllabus and various test and exam papers were scrutinised for obvious signs of male bias. Topics and problems felt to be of greater interest to girls were introduced. Strategies for involving the girls more actively in the Maths lessons were discussed and each teacher was forced to consider his or her own classroom technique. At one of these meetings, the suggestion that girls might be more successful in Maths if they were segregated from the boys was raised for the first time. Although most members of the department were sceptical about the effects of segregation, it was decided that there was nothing to lose by establishing a single all-girls set as a pilot experiment for a two year period.

Pilot scheme

Consequently, in September 1978, a single first year all-girls Maths set was established and its progress was measured against that of a group of girls of similar ability placed in a mixed Maths set. Both sets were taught similar lessons by the same teachers. By the end of the second year, it was quite apparent that most girls in the all-girls set were doing well in Maths. Mean scores on all second year Maths tests were considerably better than those of the girls in the mixed set. Furthermore, from the most superficial observation, it was apparent that the all-girls set in general was enjoying Maths. The class was lively, and there was a co-operative and harmonious atmosphere about the lessons. This pilot experiment was reported in detail by Smith (1980, 1984).

The establishment of an all-girls set had to be balanced by an all-boys Maths set. The performance of the all-boys set was never the focus of attention, for boys at Stamford

High School had a strong tradition of success in Maths and the teachers generally felt that boys would succeed equally well in single sex or co-educational sets. In the event, the mean score of the boys in the all-boys set over all the second year tests was slightly better than the mean score of boys in the equivalent mixed set.

The establishment of the two single sex sets had been accepted without question by all the boys and girls involved, and no attempt was made to discuss this arrangement with them during the two years of the pilot experiment. Nevertheless, it was quite apparent that the single sex sets in this year at least had been highly popular with boys and girls alike.

Introduction of segregated setting

The head teacher and senior staff at the school recognised that the results of this pilot experiment were far from conclusive. The number of boys and girls involved had been small and the statistics produced were clearly open to question. Nevertheless, it was felt that the results were promising enough to make a firmer commitment towards single sex setting in Maths. Accordingly, it was decided that from September 1980 all new intakes would be taught Maths in single sex sets. The performance of both boys and girls of the 1980 intake would be investigated carefully over a five year period in the hope that some firm conclusions regarding the benefits and drawbacks of single sex setting could be obtained. It was recognised that this invesigation could be of importance, for no evidence could be found of any research into the effects of single sex setting on performance in co-educational schools.

2 Design of the study

Selecting a control group

Before any assessment of the Stamford High School 1980 intake could be made, it was necessary to select a control group comprising similar boys and girls who would be taught Maths in conventional co-education sets for five years. The group selected for this purpose came from the school's 1979 intake.

The intakes of 1979 and 1980 had a great deal in common:
- They came from the same catchment area.
- They had been educated at the same group of primary schools.
- They would be taught the same number of Maths lessons per week for each of the five years.
- They would be taught Maths in sets of similar size.
- They would be taught by the same team of Maths teachers.
- They would be taught in the same suite of classrooms and use the same books and other resources.
- Additionally, they would be taught the same topics from similar schemes of work, for no major changes to the Maths curriculum were made during the period of this study.

Basis of comparison

Much of this report therefore consists of a comparison of performance in, and attitude to, Maths between pupils from the 1979 intake (henceforth referred to as 'the mixed intake') and pupils from the 1980 intake ('the segregated intake'). Boys and girls from the 1979 intake will henceforth be referred to as 'mixed boys' and 'mixed girls', and boys and girls from the 1980 intake as 'segregated boys' and 'segregated girls'.

Comparisons were carried out using:
- The Tameside Numeracy Test, taken by both intakes in the summer term of the third year.
- Four Short Maths Tests, taken by both intakes in the summer term of the fourth year.
- The APU Maths Attitude Questionnaire completed by both intakes in the summer term of the fourth year.
- The external Maths examinations taken by both intakes in the summer term of the fifth year.

These comparisons are supported by interviews with a number of girls from both intakes which were held as they approached the end of their fifth year. Additionally, six Maths teachers were interviewed towards the end of the study.

It was recognised that single sex setting was in some ways a clumsy device. The initial division of an intake into boys' sets and girls' sets reduces other possibilities in the timetable. There is less flexibility in varying set sizes for instance, and it is not as easy to break up unsuitable liaisons between pupils among the different sets. Furthermore, the sets cannot be graded as finely by ability. However, this would not be a problem in the first, second and third years at the school, for the timetable traditionally split each intake into two separate half year groups of five sets each; five boys' sets and five girls' sets would be just as flexible as this traditional division.

A more serious problem in comparing the two intakes was that comprehensive education was introduced at the school in September 1980. Consequently, the mixed intake was secondary modern and the segregated intake was comprehensive. Although the change did not completely transform the calibre of intake, the segregated boys and girls did contain both a wider range of ability and a higher proportion of more able pupils than the mixed boys and girls.

The differences in ability can be seen most clearly by comparing the breakdown of scores achieved by both intakes on NFER Test DH (Table 2.1). This well-established test of non-verbal reasoning, which is standardized over the age range 10 years 6 months to 12 years 0 months, was administered to both intakes in the October of their first term at the school.

Table 2.1 NFER test DH scores: all pupils

DH Score	Pupils Scoring Below 86	Pupils Scoring Between 86–105	Pupils Scoring Between 106–125	Pupils Scoring Above 125	'Non* Counters'	Total
Mixed boys	12	56	33	1	12	114
Segregated boys (Comprehensive)	10	45	40	7	12	114
Mixed girls	13	55	37	1	19	125
Segregated girls (Comprehensive)	4	30	44	11	24	113

* 'Non Counters' comprise absentees and pupils who joined the school after Test DH was completed.

It was decided to exclude 'Non counters' from this investigation and also pupils scoring below 86 in Test DH because their ability was extremely limited.

Matching pupils for ability

A direct comparison of all the pupils who remained would obviously be inappropriate, for it would be reasonable to expect that the segregated girls and boys would achieve higher mean scores in any Maths test because they contained a higher proportion of more able pupils. Consequently, it was decided to 'match' the pupils on the basis of individual DH scores. A 'match' comprises four pupils (one from each group) with the same or very similar DH scores. It was eventually possible to construct 65 of these 'matches' (Table 2.2).

Table 2.2 A sample of DH scores produced by the matching process

Mixed boys	Segregated boys	Mixed girls	Segregated girls
86	87	87	86
94	92	95	95
99	100	100	100
105	104	105	106
108	110	109	110
113	114	112	112
121	120	118	118
127	126	126	126

The mean scores of the four groups of 65 pupils were as follows:

Mixed boys:	105·34
Segregated boys:	105·38
Mixed girls:	105·38
Segregated girls:	105·44

Perfect matches were not possible, and it was noted that the standard deviations of the scores of the two groups of boys was slightly greater than the standard deviations of the two groups of girls. Nevertheless, the composition of the four groups of 65 pupils was statistically very similar and it would therefore be reasonable to compare the performance of any one of the groups against any of the others in Maths tests or examinations.

The major disadvantage of the matching process was that some pupils from both intakes had to be excluded from the investigation (particularly below average ability pupils from the mixed intake and above average ability from the segregated intake). Nevertheless, the pupils who remained contained an even balance across the middle ability range and an examination of the total pupil breakdown in Table 2.1 indicates that the number of pupils eliminated from the study was not excessive.

Appendix I provides more detailed information concerning Maths teaching at Stamford High School including staffing, sets and setting arrangements, curriculum and timetabling.

Appendix II contains details of significance tests and other statistical methods used in this Report.

Appendix III contains various statistical comparisons concerning the DH scores of the four groups of pupils.

3 A third year test of numeracy

The Tameside Numeracy Test

The first test available for comparison was the Tameside Numeracy Test, which was taken in identical form by both intakes during the summer terms of their third year at the school. This test comprises 112 written items divided into 13 topics (integers, fractions, decimals, percentages, volume and capacity, length, mass, money, time, area, number, tables, graphs and charts, and spatial relationships). A further eight oral items have been eliminated from this study.

As its title implies, this test is basically concerned with numeracy and the majority of questions test straightforward computational skills. The main purpose of the test is diagnostic, it being designed to expose the weaknesses of both individuals and groups of pupils. It is felt that for the purposes of this study, the total scores of pupils on the Tameside Numeracy Test can be taken as a guide to numerical ability in the third year.

Test results

The mean scores of the four groups of pupils on the Tameside Numeracy Test were as follows:

Mixed boys:	63·59
Segregated boys:	65·65
Mixed girls:	61·94
Segregated girls:	66·03

Differences between the mean scores of mixed boys and mixed girls and between the mean scores of segregated boys and segregated girls were quite small, but the segregated boys and segregated girls each had higher mean scores than mixed boys and mixed girls respectively. The greatest difference lay between the segregated girls and mixed girls. When the four sets of scores were compared statistically, however, none of the differences was significant.

The test results were next analysed by topic and it was found that segregated girls did better than mixed girls on eleven of the thirteen topics, and on six of these topics (decimals, volume and capacity, money, time, number and spatial relationships), the differences were statistically significant.

These results suggest that the girls of the segregated intake did benefit from being taught Maths separately from boys in their first three years at least as far as basic numeracy is concerned.

The general superiority of the performance of the segregated girls can be clearly seen in Figure 3.1(b). Each plot on the figure represents a separate item on the test. Plots in the bottom left hand corner of the figure represent items which few pupils answered correctly, and plots in the top right hand corner represent items answered correctly by most pupils. The vertical axis represents the percentage of segregated girls answering each item correctly, and the horizontal axis represents the percentage of mixed girls answering correctly. Plots above the diagonal line represent the questions which a higher percentage of segregated girls answered correctly, and these heavily outnumber the plots below the diagonal line.

Segregated boys did better than mixed boys on nine of the 13 topics, but only on spatial relationships was the difference statistically significant. These differences were not sufficient to conclude that segregated boys had gained any benefit from being taught separately from girls.

Relative difficulty of topics The 13 topics were next ranked in terms of their relative difficulty for each of the four groups concerned. Relative difficulty was assessed by ranking the mean percentage score for each topic. The results are displayed in Table 3.1.

Table 3.1 Tameside Numeracy Test: Relative difficulty of topics

Rank (1 = most difficult)	Mixed boys	Segregated boys	Mixed girls	Segregated girls
1	Percentages	Percentages	Percentages	Percentages
2	Fractions	Fractions	Fractions	Fractions
3	Decimals	Decimals	Decimals	Decimals
4	Spatial relationships	Area	Spatial relationships	Area
5	Area	Length	Length	Spatial relationships
6	Length	Mass	Area	Length
7	Mass	Spatial relationships	Mass	Mass
8	Volume and capacity	Number	Volume and capacity	Volume and capacity
9	Time	Time	Number	Time
10	Number	Money	Time	Integers
11	Money	Volume and capacity	Money	Number
12	Tables/graphs/charts	Integers	Intergers	Tables/graphs/charts
13	Integers	Tables/graphs/charts	Tables/graphs/charts	Money

Figure 3.1 Tameside Numeracy Test: item by item comparisons of performance.

a Mixed boys and segregated boys

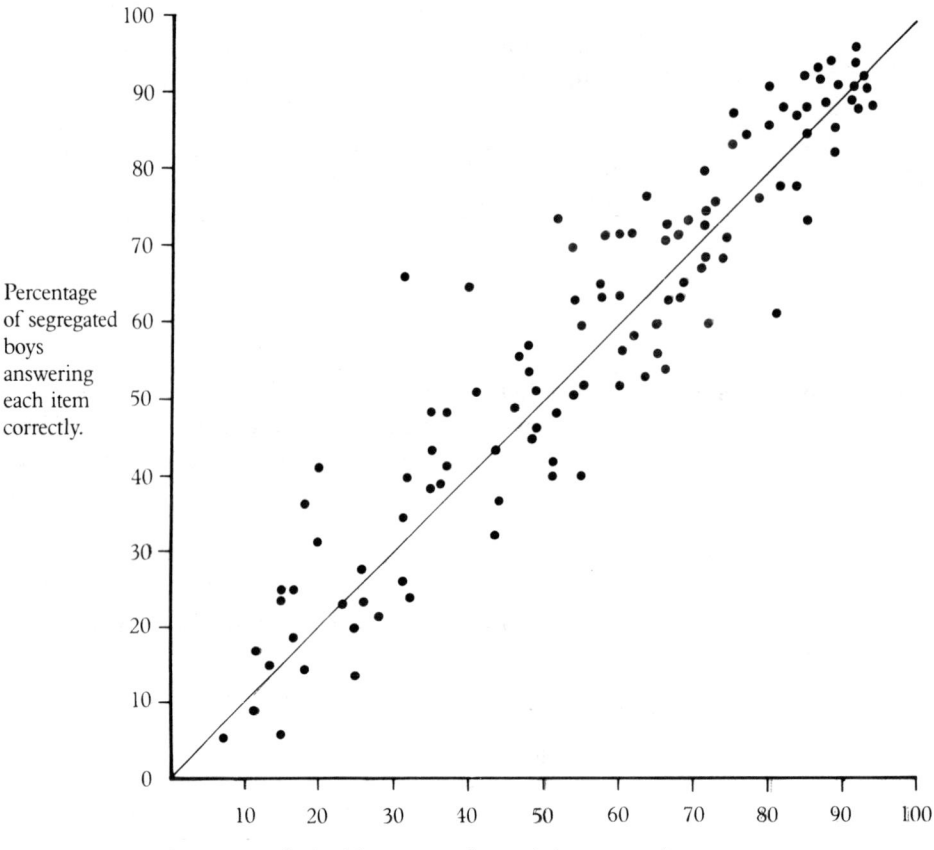

b Mixed girls and segregated girls

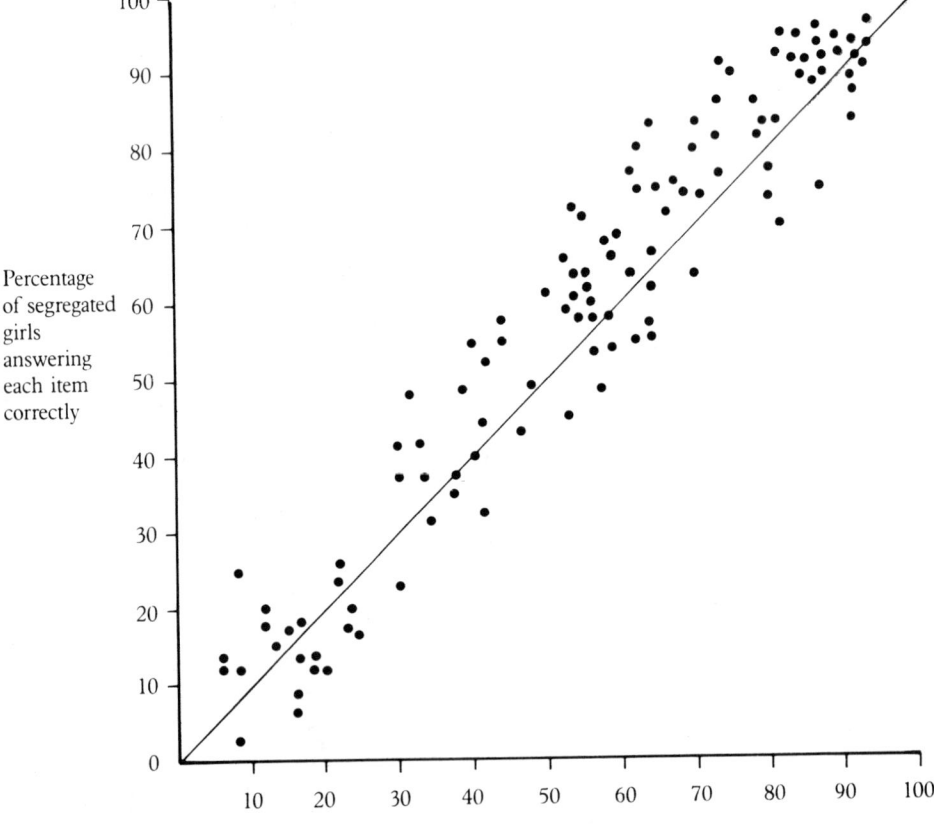

c Mixed boys and mixed girls

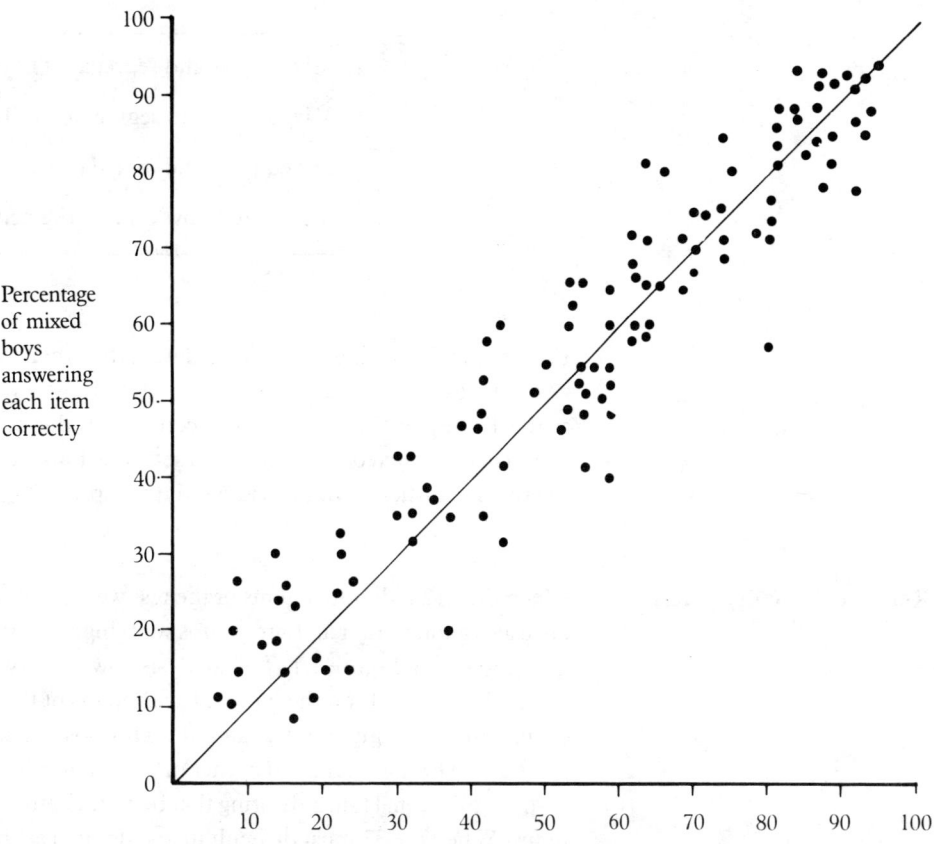

Percentage of mixed girls answering each item correctly.

d Segregated boys and segregated girls

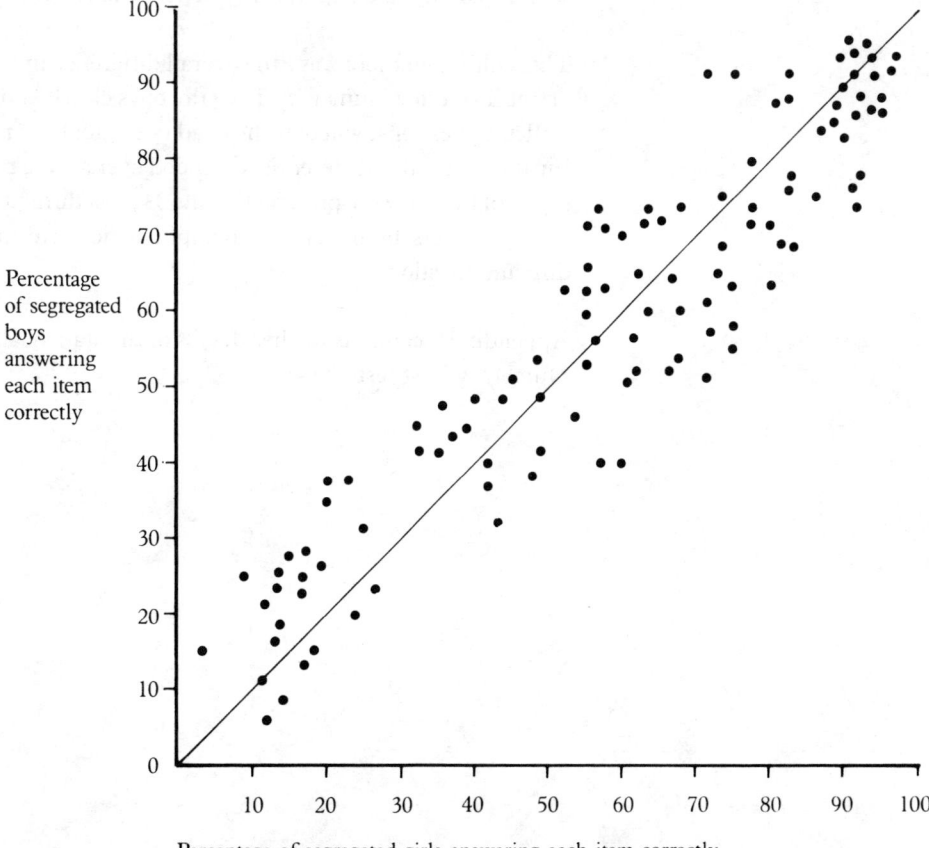

Percentage of segregated girls answering each item correctly.

Note:
Each plot on the figures represents the performance of the two groups on one item of the tests.

The Spearman correlation coefficients for the various pairs of groups were as follows:

Mixed boys and segregated boys:	0·92
Mixed girls and segregated girls:	0·95
Mixed boys and mixed girls:	0·98
Segregated boys and segregated girls:	0·90

Each group is very highly correlated with the others, all four groups finding percentages, fractions and decimals to be the most difficult topics (in that order). As far as the Tameside Numeracy Test is concerned, these results suggest that neither sex difference nor mixed and segregated setting arrangements had any appreciable effect on the relative difficulty of individual Maths topics.

Relative difficulty of items

When the 112 individual items of the test were analysed in terms of difficulty, it was once again found that all four groups were highly correlated: indeed, this is apparent from a glance at Figure 3.1. This analysis however revealed that both groups of boys did better than the girls on the more difficult items of the test. This can be seen from an examination of Figures 3.1(c) and (d). The most difficult items are indicated by the plots in the bottom left hand corner of each figure. In both cases, these plots cluster above the diagonal line indicating that boys did better than girls on the majority of these items. When the 33 most difficult items (defined as those items which less than 50% of pupils in each group answered correctly) were separated from the rest, it was found that the mixed boys did significantly better than the mixed girls and that similarly, the segregated boys did significantly better than the segregated girls.

Thus, although there was little overall difference in the performance of boys and girls on the Tameside Numeracy Test, the boys clearly did better at answering the more difficult questions, whether they had been taught in mixed or segregated sets. Furthermore, this differential extended over a wide range of topics, for 10 of the 13 topics of the test were presented in the 33 most difficult questions. The establishment of segregated sets did not appear to improve the performance of the girls on the more difficult questions.

Appendix IV contains further details of the statistical analysis of the Tameside Numeracy Test results.

4 Maths performance in the fourth year

Four short tests

During the last three weeks of the fourth year at the school, each of the two intakes attempted four short Maths tests. The four tests were designed to supplement the Tameside Numeracy Test. They were intended to be more searching than the Tameside Numeracy Test and included many items requiring problem solving skills. Several items were derived from the tests used in the APU Secondary Surveys of Mathematical Development. The remainder were devised by the recently retired Head of Maths at the school. The tests were not standardised, but to eliminate errors and ambiguities a trial was conducted with a small number of fourth year pupils from another secondary school.

The tests were taken during the course of ordinary Maths lessons and they were taken in identical form by both intakes. Maths teachers were asked to ensure that all pupils were given sufficient time for each test (it was expected that slower pupils might require 15–20 minutes for each test). Not more than two tests were to be taken in a Maths lesson of 70 minutes.

Test results

Table 4.1 shows that mixed boys performed better than mixed girls on all four of the tests and when the total scores of these two groups of pupils were compared, the difference was highly significant and could be taken to suggest that the mixed boys would do better than the mixed girls in the external Maths examinations in the fifth year. It should be stressed that there was nothing particularly remarkable about these two sets of scores, for boys normally perform better than girls in fourth year Maths tests and examinations at the school. The main point of interest lay in whether the segregated girls could improve on the performance of the mixed girls and in effect they failed to do so for when the total scores of the two groups of girls were compared statistically, the difference was well below the level of significance. The mean scores of both groups of girls on the four individual tests were mostly below those of both groups of boys.

Table 4.1 Four short tests: mean scores, by group

	Maximum score	Mean scores			
		Mixed boys	Segregated boys	Mixed girls	Segregated girls
Test 1 (geometry)	13	7·3	7·2	6·1	6·4
Test 2 (proportion, rates, ratio)	8	4·5	3·9	4·0	3·5
Test 3 (mensuration)	8	3·5	3·2	2·5	2·8
Test 4 (algebra)	14	7·3	7·5	7·1	7·2
Total	43	22·6	21·8	19·7	19·9

Figure 4.1
Four short tests: item by item comparisons of performance
a   Mixed boys and segregated boys

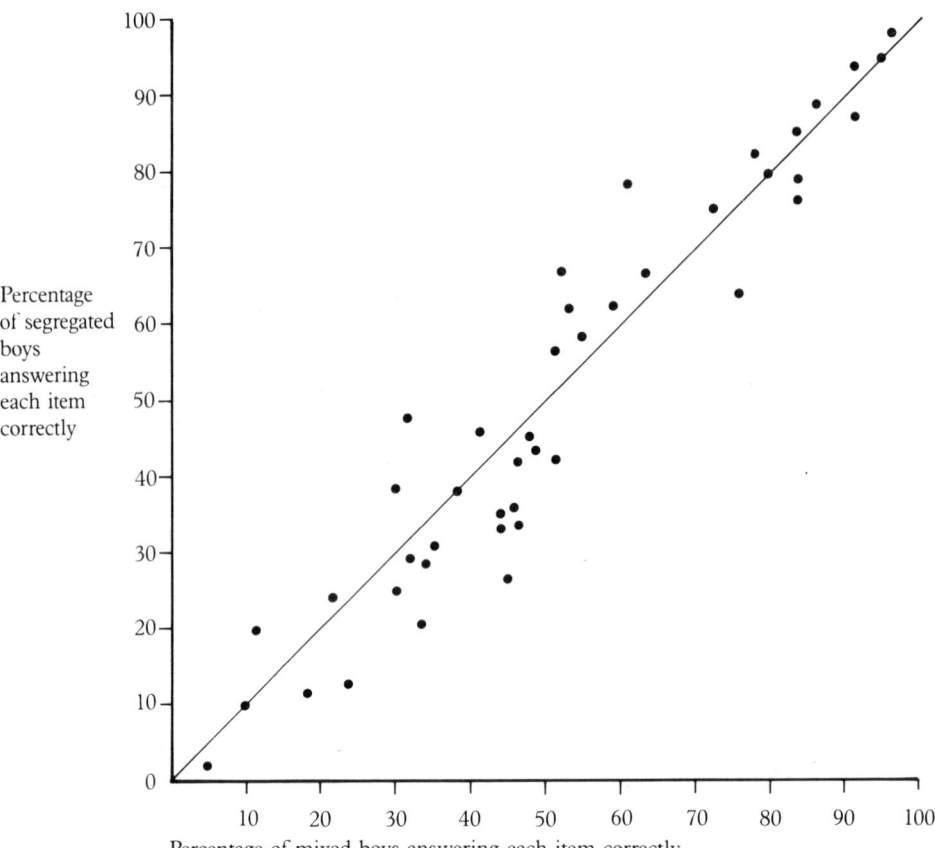

b   Mixed girls and segregated girls

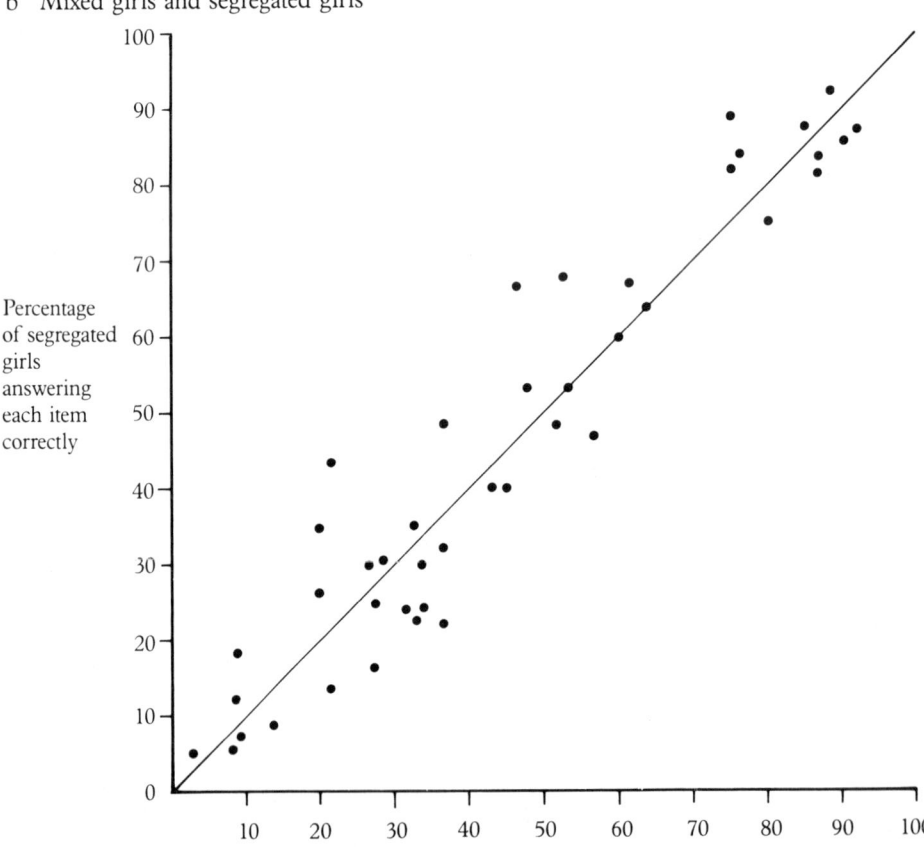

c Mixed boys and mixed girls

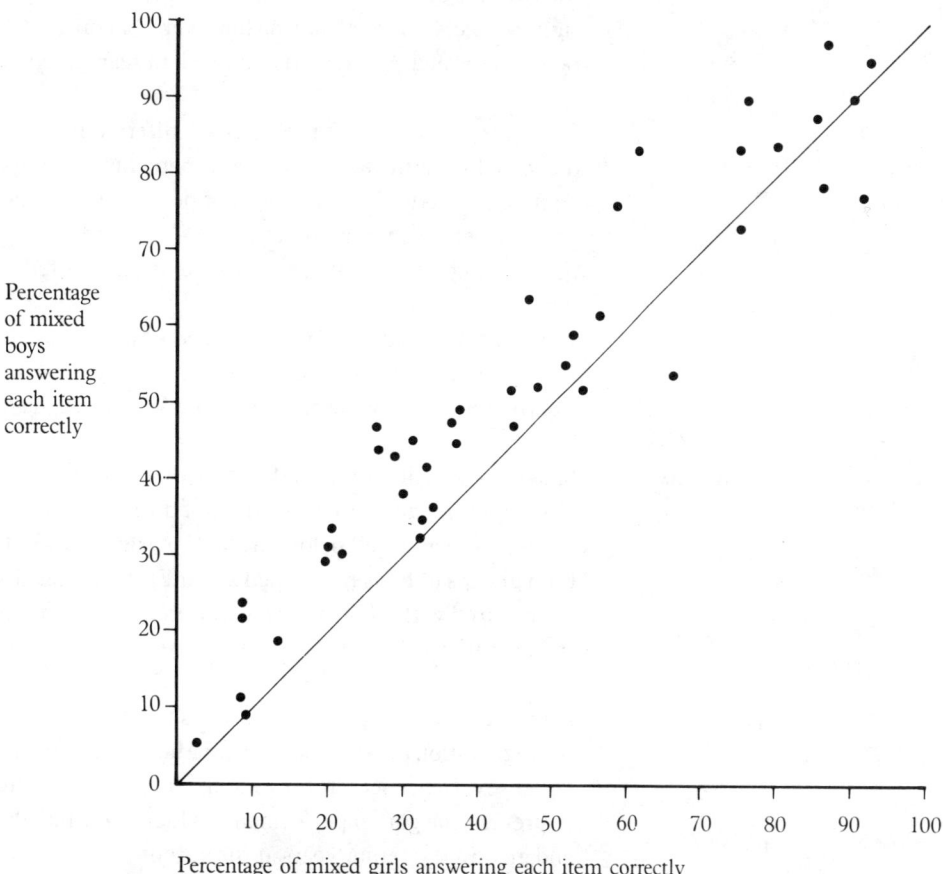

d Segregated boys and segregated girls

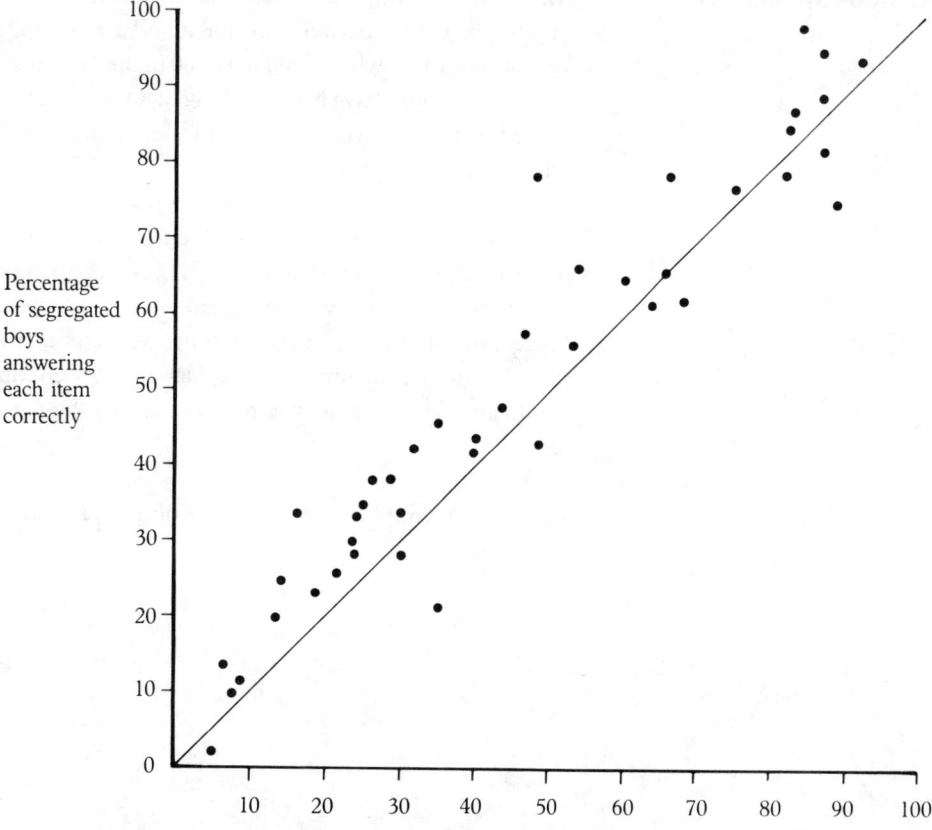

Note:
Each plot on the figures represents the performance of the two groups on one item of the tests.

The mixed boys achieved a higher total mean score than the segregated boys, but when the two sets of scores were tested, the difference was again well below the level of significance. It is worth noting however, that on Test 2 (proportion, rates, ratio) mixed boys performed significantly better than segregated boys.

In Figure 4.1, each plot represents a different item on the four tests, and a plot on a diagonal line indicates that the same percentage of pupils from two groups has answered an item correctly. The similarity of performance of both groups of boys and of both groups of girls can be seen in Figures 4.1(a) and 4.1(b) respectively. In both figures, the plots are highly correlated and are evenly distributed on both sides of the diagonal line.

Figures 4.1(c) and (d) compare mixed boys with mixed girls and segregated boys with segregated girls respectively. The superiority in performance of both groups of boys is clearly indicated by the clustering of plots above the diagonal line in both figures.

When the sets of scores on the individual tests were examined, it was noted that although both groups of girls did not do as well as the boys on Test 4 (algebra), the differences were well below the level of significance. On the other three tests however, both groups of boys performed significantly better than the two groups of girls they were paired with. The differences were greatest in Test 1 (geometry) and Test 3 (mensuration).

All these results suggest that as far as the work covered by the four tests is concerned, the segregation of boys and girls for Maths had little if any effect on the performance of either sex. In particular, the establishment of segregated girls sets had apparently failed to prevent the gap in performance which traditionally develops in Maths between boys and girls in the senior years at the school.

Analysis by ability group

An additional comparison was made between the less able pupils (defined as those pupils who scored between 86–100 on NFER Test DH in the first year) and the more able pupils (those who scored over 100 in the same test). The great majority of the more able pupils would have been working in 'O' level or CSE maths sets from the beginning of the fourth year, whereas many of the less able pupils would be in non-exam Maths sets.

It was found that among the less able pupils, both mixed girls and segregated girls performed almost as well as the boys they were paired with; it was the more able girls who performed badly when compared with the boys. These results could therefore suggest that most of the more able boys were coping well with external exam work, and many of the girls of apparently similar ability were finding this work difficult. This would appear to be true whether boys or girls had been taught in mixed or segregated sets.

Appendix V contains further details of the statistical analysis of the results of the four short tests.

5 Pupils' attitudes towards Maths

The APU Mathematics Attitude Questionnaire

During the period that each of the two intakes were attempting the four short tests (the last three weeks of the summer term of the fourth year), the pupils were also asked to complete the APU Mathematics Attitude Questionnaire. This questionnaire was developed from the second and third of three Secondary Surveys of Mathematical Development conducted by the National Foundation for Educational Research on behalf of the Assessment of Performance Unit. These surveys were designed to present a national picture of mathematical performance of 15 year olds, and the attitude questionnaire was ideal for the purpose of this investigation.

The questionnaire was completed at the school during normal Maths lessons. Although no time limit was set, it was found that a lesson of 70 minutes was quite long enough for completion.

The questionnaire is divided into four sections, but only the responses to the first two (Parts A and B) have been analysed for this report. Part A is a series of statements expressing feelings about how difficult, useful and enjoyable Maths is, as a school subject. Pupils are asked to rate the degree to which they agree with each statement, and each response is scored on a five point scale. Part B is a list of Maths topics. Pupils are asked to express the degree to which they find each topic useful and difficult. The responses are scored on a three point scale, and each topic can be ranked by both usefulness and difficulty.

Difficulty

There are 17 separate statements concerned with the difficulty of Maths, and as each statement is scored on the scale of one to five, the total score range is 17 to 85. A high individual difficulty score indicates that the pupil perceives Maths as a difficult subject, and a low score indicates the pupil perceives Maths as relatively easy.

The mean scores of the four groups of pupils were as follows:

Mixed boys	46·70
Segregated boys	47·73
Mixed girls	54·23
Segregated girls	54·16

The differences between the sets of scores of the two groups of boys and between the sets of scores of the two groups of girls did not reach the level of statistical significance which suggests that the establishment of single sex sets for Maths had very little or no effect on either boys' or girls' perception of the difficulty of the subject.

When the sets of scores of the two groups of boys were compared with the sets of scores of both groups of girls however, the differences were highly significant. Girls apparently regard Maths as a more difficult subject than boys whether they have been taught Maths in single sex sets or not. Table 5.1 illustrates these differences.

Table 5.1 Difficulty statements in which the difference between the responses of boys and girls was significant

Difficulty statement	Pupil groups	Strongly agree %	Agree %	Undecided %	Disagree %	Strongly disagree %
When it comes to doing a problem in Maths, I get all the formulas mixed up.	Mixed boys	9	30	14	42	5
	Mixed girls	8	59	6	27	0
	Segregated boys	5	38	3	48	7
	Segregated girls	5	49	20	23	3
Maths is easy for me.	Mixed boys	5	17	14	45	19
	Mixed girls	0	5	12	67	16
	Segregated boys	5	23	18	41	13
	Segregated girls	2	8	10	54	26
I'm surprised if I get a lot of Maths right.	Mixed boys	5	19	3	64	9
	Mixed girls	11	45	8	31	5
In lots of Maths, it's hard to know what's being asked of you.	Mixed boys	5	34	17	42	2
	Mixed girls	6	63	19	9	3
I can do the work in class, but I don't know how to apply it.	Mixed boys	2	28	20	45	5
	Mixed girls	5	59	16	20	0
Each year Maths becomes more difficult to understand.	Segregated boys	8	48	3	36	5
	Segregated girls	25	44	8	18	5

When the individual difficulty scores of the mixed girls were compared with the mixed boys with whom they were paired, it was found that the differences were greater among the more able pupils (those with DH scores over 100) than among the less able. A similar pattern was found when the paired difficulty scores of segregated girls and segregated boys were compared.

Thus a picture emerges of the majority of the more able boys at the school being relatively successful and self-confident at Maths, whereas many of their female counterparts were less successful and perceived Maths as a more difficult subject. Single sex sets had apparently failed to improve either the performance or the self-confidence of the more able girls.

When pupil responses to the relative difficulty of individual Maths topics were analysed, it was found that there were sufficient responses to measure 24 of the 27 topics on the questionnaire.

Mixed girls found 17 of the 24 topics more difficult than mixed boys, but only in two of these topics (geometrical constructions and scale problems) were the differences significant.

Segregated girls found 18 of the 24 topics more difficult than segregated boys and in six of these topics (geometrical constructions, adding or subtracting decimals, scale problems, measuring angles, multiplying or dividing decimals and reflections or rotations) the differences were significant.

It is interesting to note that both groups of girls regarded geometrical constructions and scale problems much more difficult than the two groups of boys. This could well be related to the fact that most boys in both groups were studying technical drawing for external examinations whereas most girls had chosen not to study technical drawing.

The 24 topics were ranked in order of difficulty for each of the four groups of pupils and the following correlation co-efficients (Spearman) were calculated:

Mixed boys and segregated boys:	0·87
Mixed girls and segregated girls:	0·82
Mixed boys and mixed girls:	0·89
Segregated boys and segregated girls:	0·72

These results are similar to the difficulty correlations reported in Chapter 3 in that each group is highly correlated with the others, but the difference between the correlation co-efficients of mixed boys and mixed girls on the one hand and segregated boys and segregated girls on the other is large enough in this case to suggest that co-educational sets may have some effect in reducing differences in the perception of the difficulty of individual Maths topics between boys and girls.

Utility

There are ten separate statements on the attitude questionnaire related to utility, and as each statement is scored on the scale 1 to 5, the score range is 10 to 50. A high individual utility score indicates that the pupil perceives maths as a very useful school subject.

The mean scores of the four groups of pupils were as follows:

Mixed boys:	34·44
Segregated boys:	34·44
Mixed girls:	34·33
Segregated girls:	31·97

These figures indicate that segregated girls regarded Maths as a less useful subject than the other three groups of pupils.

When the four sets of utility scores were compared, it was found that the differences between the segregated girls and each of the other three groups of pupils were significant. Table 5.2 illustrates some of these differences.

Table 5.2 Utility statements in which there were significant differences between segregated girls and other groups of pupils

Utility statement	Pupil group	Strongly Agree %	Agree %	Undecided %	Disagree %	Strongly Disagree %
Knowing Maths is helpful in understanding today's world.	Segregated boys	37	41	5	14	3
	Segregated girls	16	51	10	23	0
I don't find much use for Maths outside school.	Mixed girls	2	23	3	45	27
	Segregated girls	10	35	5	33	17
Most people only need to learn enough Maths to take care of their money.	Mixed girls	3	27	4	50	16
	Segregated girls	8	44	7	23	18

When the individual utility scores of the segregated girls were compared with both mixed girls and segregated boys, it was found that the differences were greater among the more able pupils. This suggests that more able girls are likely to develop a lower perception of the utility of Maths if they are taught in segregated sets.

Enjoyment

There are seven separate statements concerned with the enjoyment of Maths, and the total enjoyment score range is seven to 35. A high individual enjoyment score indicates the pupil enoys Maths as a school subject, and a low score indicates dislike of Maths.

The mean scores of the four groups of pupils were as follows:

Mixed boys:	20·83
Segregated boys:	21·86
Mixed girls:	20·20
Segregated girls:	19·39

The mean scores of the two groups of girls were lower than the mean scores of the two groups of boys, but when the sets of scores were tested, the only significant difference was between segregated girls and segregated boys (see table 5.3).

Table 5.3 Enjoyment statement in which the difference between the responses of segregated boys and segregated girls was significant

Enjoyment statement	Pupil group	Strongly Agree %	Agree %	Undecided %	Disagree %	Strongly Disagree %
I like Maths because I have to work things out.	Segregated boys	10	49	10	26	5
	Segregated girls	5	26	21	41	7

When the individual enjoyment scores of the segregated girls were compared with the segregated boys they were paired with, it was found that the differences were greater among the more able pupils. In other words, the pattern was similar to that revealed by the comparisons of the difficulty and utility scores. The low scores of segregated girls on the enjoyment scale apparently contrast sharply with the popularity of Maths observed among the segregated girls of the pilot experiment (see Chapter 1). It should be pointed out that the latter group were in the first and second year when these observations were made whereas the girls who completed the questionnaire were at the end of their fourth year at the school.

The mean scores of the four groups of pupils on all three of the scales measured by the APU questionnaire indicate that the two groups of boys displayed a more positive attitude to Maths than the two groups of girls. The differences between boys and girls were greater on the difficulty scale than on the utility and enjoyment scales and these results were in line with those obtained by the APU using a very similar set of attitude statements in the Third Secondary Survey of Mathematical Development (1982).

The responses of both groups of boys were similar on all three attitude scales, and the responses of both groups of girls were similar on the difficulty and enjoyment scales. On balance, therefore, these responses suggest that segregated Maths classes have not been a major influence in determining the attitudes of boys and girls to Maths (although it was noted that the segregated girls perceived Maths as a less useful subject than the other three group of pupils).

Appendix VI contains further details of the statistical analysis of the APU Mathematics Attitude Questionnaire.

6 External examination results

The examinations

At the beginning of the fourth year, all those pupils who had performed well in Maths in the third year from both the mixed and segregated intakes began two-year Maths courses leading to either the 'O' level or 16+ examinations (in which pupils are awarded either 'O' Level or CSE Grades according to performance). The next group began courses leading to the CSE Maths examinations, and finally a minority of low achievers were placed on a non-examination course.

Examination results

The Maths external examinations were taken by both intakes in the summer term of the fifth year and the detailed results of the four groups of pupils are recorded in table 6.1.

Table 6.1 Maths external examination results: Detailed breakdown

Exam Grade Achieved	GCE grade 'A'	GCE grade 'B'	GCE grade 'C' or CSE grade 1	GCE grade 'D' or CSE grade 2	GCE grade 'E' or CSE grade 3	CSE grade 4	CSE grade 5	CSE Unclassified	Absent	Did Not Enter	Total
Mixed Boys	1	4	15	8	12	12	2	1	2	8	65
Segregated boys	3	4	9	5	12	19	4	2	2	5	65
Mixed girls	1	2	8	7	10	16	5	3	2	11*	65
Segregated girls	1	5	6	8	5	17	14	2	3	4	65

* One girl from the mixed intake left the school in November of her fifth year. As she belonged to a non-exam Maths set, she has been placed in the 'Did Not Enter' column. The remainder of the pupils of all four groups were on the register of the school at least until they were legally old enough to leave school.

For the purposes of statistical comparison, this detailed breakdown was simplified by placing all of the pupils in one of three classifications:

Classification A: Pupils who reached an acceptable 'O' level standard in Maths by obtaining an 'O' level grade 'A', 'B' or 'C' or a CSE grade 1.

Classification B: Pupils who gained a useful Maths qualification below an acceptable 'O' level standard by obtaining an 'O' level grade 'D' or 'E' or a CSE grade 2, 3 or 4.

Classification C: Pupils who left school with a Maths qualification of little value (CSE grade 5) or no Maths qualification at all.

This simplified breakdown is displayed in table 6.2. This table reveals that the examination results achieved by the two groups of boys were very similar, and when these two sets of results were compared statistically, the difference was well below any acceptable level of significance.

Table 6.2 Maths external examination results: Simplified breakdown

Examination grade achieved	GCE grades 'A' 'B', or 'C' or CSE grade 1 No.	%	GCE grades 'D' or 'E' or CSE grades, 2, 3, or 4 No.	%	CSE grade 5 or unclassified or absent or did not enter No.	%	Total (= 100%)
Mixed boys	20	31%	32	49%	13	20%	65
Segregated boys	16	25%	36	55%	13	20%	65
Mixed girls	11	17%	33	51%	21	32%	65
Segregated girls	12	18%	30	46%	23	35%	65

The examination results achieved by the two groups of girls were also very similar, and when these two sets of results were compared statistically, the difference was even smaller than that between the two groups of boys.

These comparisons indicate that single sex setting for Maths had had little effect on the examination performance of either the segregated boys or the segregated girls as groups of pupils. It is possible that the examination performance of individual pupils may have been helped or hindered by segregation, but the overall results of the four groups of pupils suggest that the performance of the majority of boys and girls was little affected by mixed or single sex setting.

When the examination results of the two groups of boys were compared with the results of the two groups of girls, it was quite apparent that the two boys' groups had been more successful. Both groups of boys achieved more acceptable 'O' level Maths passes than either group of girls and more girls from both groups left school with a low qualification or no qualification in Maths than did so from either group of boys.

Nevertheless, the differences between the examination results of the mixed boys and mixed girls and between the examination results of the segregated boys and segregated girls were not significant at the 5% level (although they were close to significance at the 10% level).

Figure 6.1 compares the examination result of each individual girl with the individual boy she was paired with by ability.

Figure 6.1

External examination results analysis by paired pupils
a   Mixed boys and mixed girls

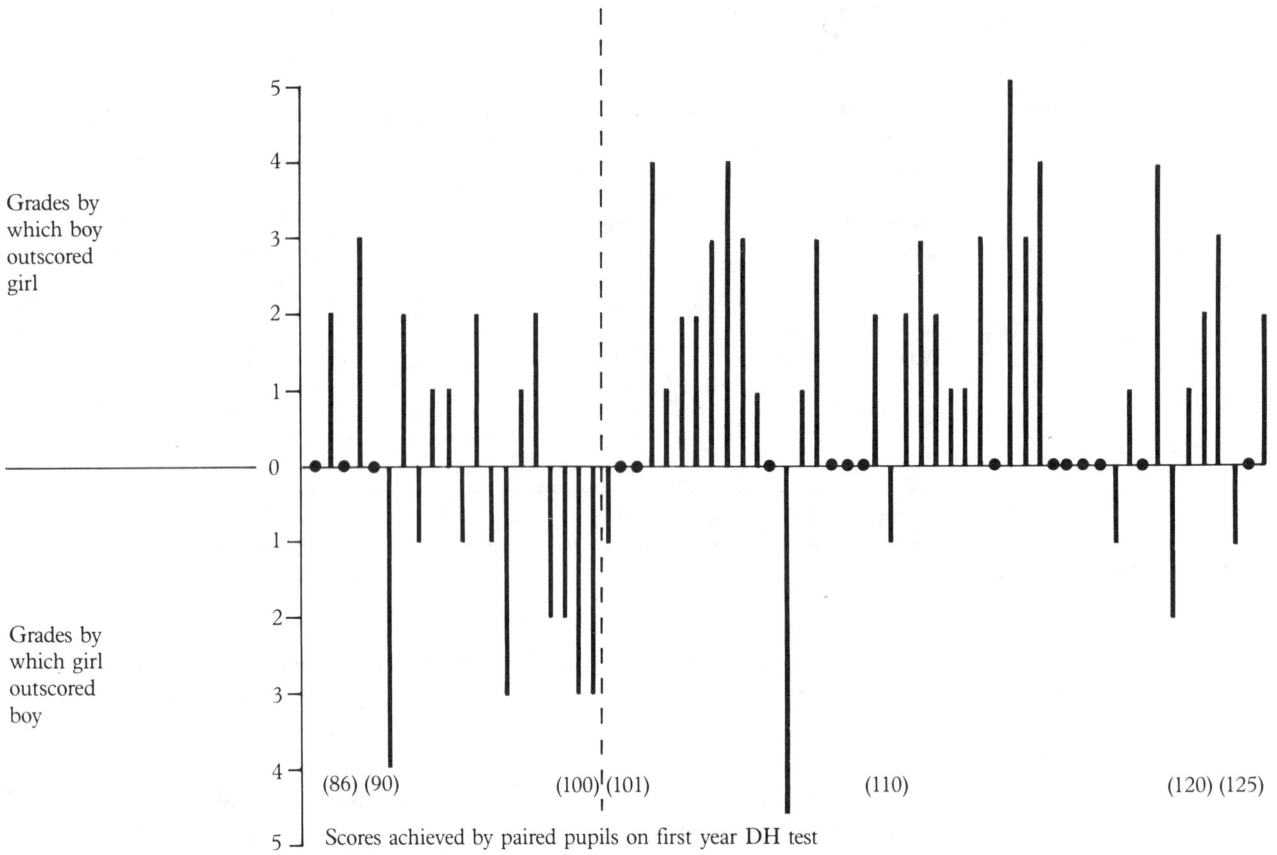

b   Segregated boys and segregated girls

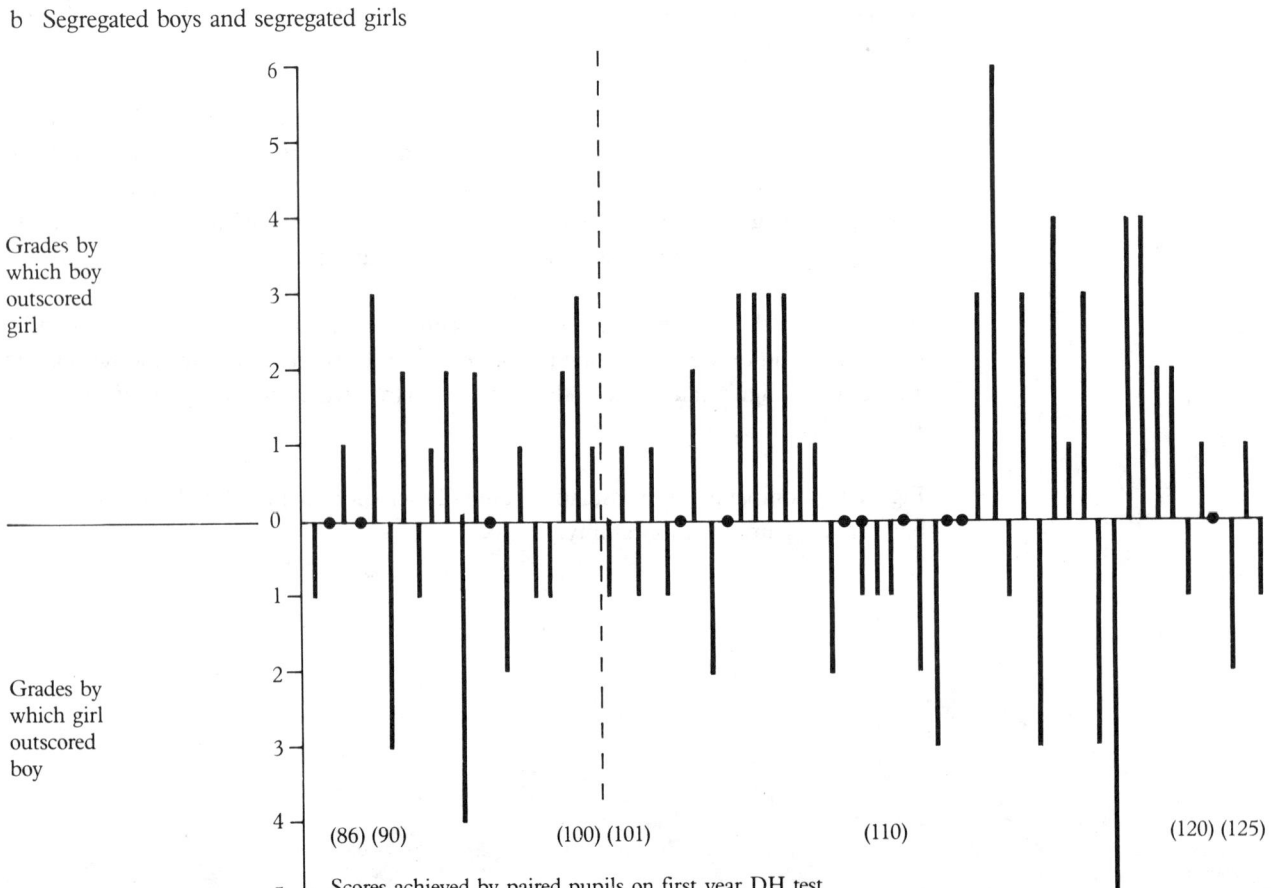

28

The relationship between the examination results of mixed boys and mixed girls is illustrated in figure 6.1(a) and that between segregated boys and segregated girls in figure 6.1(b). The superior performance of the two boys' groups can be recognised by the perpendiculars rising from the horizontal line which outnumber the perpendiculars falling from the horizontal line in each figure. In figure 6.1(a), it is apparent that the examination results of the less able boys and girls (those pupils who scored between 86–100 on the DH Test in the first year) were very similar. Among the more able pupils (those with DH scores over 100), however, the difference in the examination results was considerable. A similar pattern can be detected in figure 6.1(b), although it is less clearly marked.

Comparison with fourth year performance

Finally, the examination results of the four groups of pupils were very similar in pattern to the results which the four groups obtained in the four short tests at the end of the fourth year. This suggests not only that performance in the four short tests was a good predictor of performance in the external examinations, but also that the relative performances between boys and girls and between mixed and segregated pupils had been clearly established before the fifth year; apparently nothing happened in the fifth year to change markedly these relationships.

7   Girls who find Maths difficult

Mixed Girls

Possibly the most interesting point to emerge from the first analysis of responses of the mixed intake of the APU Mathematics Attitude Questionnaire was the large number of girls who perceived Maths as a difficult subject. The contrast with the boys was particularly marked among average and above-average ability pupils. As a result it was decided to interview a group of mixed girls who regarded Maths as a difficult subject. At the time of the interviews the mixed intake was in the second term of its fifth year the school.

The main purposes of the interviews were first to establish when the girls began to regard Maths as difficult subject and second to investigate whether the presence of boys in Maths had contributed to their difficulties.

Fifteen girls were selected for interview. All of these girls had been regarded as being of average or above average ability in the first year, for they had all achieved scores over 100 on the DH non-verbal reasoning test. Additionally, they had all recorded scores over 60 on the difficulty scale of the attitude questionnaire. Finally, the list of girls had been screened by the pastoral staff at the school; all of the girls selected were believed to have stable home backgrounds, and none of them had a serious disciplinary record at the school. All fifteen of the girls selected agreed to be interviewed.

In the week before the interviews began, the girls were asked to complete a short questionnaire which had been designed to focus their attention on some of the themes to be discussed in the interviews. It was not intended that the completed questionnaires would be subjected to serious statistical analysis, but some of the responses were particularly interesting.

The interviews indicated that only two of the 15 girls associated their first difficulties in Maths with primary school. One of these had always found Maths difficult and the other had had a serious personality clash with one of her teachers and for a time had virtually ceased to make any effort in lessons at all. She later found she had serious problems in making up lost ground in Maths.

The remaining girls generally expressed both an enjoyment of Maths and an ability to cope with the work both in Junior school and in the first year at Stamford High School.

Dorothy: 'Yes, I enjoyed it then. He went through it dead good. Thorough like. I could understand it then.'

The 'thoroughness' which Dorothy referred to is an important element in the teaching of first year Maths at the school. As the pupils are drawn from a large number of feeder primary schools, the quality of Maths teaching they have received, and the range of topics they have covered varies considerably. Consequently, a great deal of consolidation is necessary when they begin secondary education.

The Maths reports which each of the girls received at the end of the first year support the view that they were mainly coping well at this stage. Most of the girls were said to have settled down well and were making good progress.

It became quite clear from the interviews that the majority of the girls began to regard Maths as a difficult subject sometime between the early part of the second year and the early part of the fourth year (when the external exam courses began). The girls frequently identified their difficulties with a change of teacher.

Sally: 'Yes, and then in the second year we started having Teacher X and it started getting difficult. At first we did similar stuff what we had with Teacher Y. Then we started moving on. You go over things too quick. We'd no sooner start one thing than we'd move on to another thing. And then those that are dragging behind, he sort of leaves them dragging behind.'

Barbara: 'I don't know, the teacher wasn't explaining enough. Mind you, Teacher Z went through things again and again, but Teacher A just explains once, then tells you to do it. I need to be told over and over again before I get it.'

Jane: 'Yes. I think (pause), I think for me we began to move too fast in the fourth year. I just begin to grasp something, then we have to move on. Last year, it was very hard. We were pushed and pushed, we moved so fast. I couldn't really grasp anything.'

The problem of speed bothered most of the girls as is clear from their responses to the following statement:

	Strongly agree	Agree	Undecided	Disagree	Strongly disagree
We go on to new work in Maths far too quickly for me.	6	7	2	0	0

One girl made the interesting suggestion that the speed with which they moved on to new topics was associated with the behaviour of the boys.

Dawn: 'Well, they (the boys) muck and mess about. They always want to talk. So we have to change about. The topics and that. When the boys have finished their work, we move on to something new whether we've finished or not.'

Despite Dawn's comment, it was apparent that almost all the girls primarily associated their difficulties with an inability to comprehend much of the work in Maths lessons. Some of the girls regarded the presence of boys as an additional factor which compounded their problems, but other were quite content to be in mixed classes.

	Strongly agree	Agree	Undecided	Disagree	Strongly disagree
I think I would do better if there were no boys in my Maths class.	1	7	1	4	2

The girls who would have preferred single sex Maths classes sometimes complained that the boys were not serious enough.

Audrey: 'Well, they don't buckle down to their work as well as girls do. The girls try to do it. And the boys often just mess about. And talk and that.'

Audrey was one of the girls who had apparently suffered most from the presence of boys in Maths. Like most of the girls, however, she had enjoyed Maths in the first year.

Audrey: 'I think it was the fact that there weren't many boys in our set. And we got on better with it being a woman teacher. There was a good relationship. She's always like that. Nice. And there weren't many boys. Only three or four. I find if there aren't many boys about, I work a lot better.'

She was asked later when she became conscious of boys in Maths.

Audrey: 'I think (pause) late third year, early fourth year. (pause) Because they started opening their mouths then. If they got something wrong they'd say something. And they behaved worse. And I stopped asking questions because they always had something to say.'

Interviewer: 'What sort of things might they say?'

Audrey: ' "Oh, can't you do it? Anyone can do that. You must be right thick". And I felt embarrassed.'

Audrey was by no means the only girl who wouldn't ask for help in class.

Barbara: 'Maths would be better with no boys. Most girls you know won't tell Sir if they haven't understood. They won't tell him. I don't care whether lads laugh or not. The other girls easy get upset. They won't ask. They stay quiet.'

Barbara went on to say that she felt that her Maths teacher gave more attention to the boys than the girls, but in this she was in a minority. Almost all the girls believed that the teachers tried to devote equal attention to both sexes. Indeed, they were generally complimentary about all their Maths teachers and they recognised the problems which teachers faced in the classroom.

Almost without exception, whether they were in favour of segregated Maths classes or not, the girls were critical of boys' behaviour. The following comments came from a girl who approved of mixed Maths sets:

Sally: 'I suppose you've got to get used to mixing haven't you? If you're with girls all the time, then you're in a situation where you're with boys, you'd be sort of shy with them being there. It all depends on what sort of boys they are. If they're loud and noisy, I just ignore them or tell them to shut up, you know. But most of them in our set are quiet, so it's all right.'

Sally was later asked why she had requested a demotion to a lower set at the end of the second year. After stating that she was near the bottom of her set she went on:

Sally: 'And I didn't get on with the people in the top set. It were A.... B...., he used to sit behind me, poking me, calling me names and everything.'

There was almost no positive communication between any of the girls interviewed and the boys in their Maths classes. Each girl generally sat with a close friend in a cluster of girls. The girls frequently helped each other with the work, and did not appear to involve the boys in this activity.

Joan: 'Well, it just doesn't bother me. I pay no attention to them (the boys). I just get on with my work. The only people I talk to are the girls around me.'

Sally: 'Well, I suppose, well in the lessons girls just talk to girls don't they? I talk quite a bit to the four girls who sit behind the empty desk. I sometimes talk to them, but mostly I just talk to Lynn.'

Segregated girls

In the winter of 1985 it was decided to interview a group of girls from the segregated intake who perceived Maths as a difficult subject. The same criteria to those used in selecting the mixed girls were applied, and eventually 10 segregated girls were interviewed. The preliminary questionnaire used with the mixed girls was not given to the segregated girls (for many of the questions were not appropriate to this group).

The main purpose in interviewing the ten girls was to examine their opinions of single sex setting in Maths. At the time of their interviews, the girls were all approaching the end of their five years at the school and thus had considerable experience of single sex lessons in Maths. Furthermore, they would be able to compare this experience to lessons with boys in all other academic subjects.

All ten girls were asked whether in general they felt that single sex setting in Maths had been a good idea or not and they responded as follows:

In favour	Undecided	Against
6	1	3

This result was probably in line with the opinions of all the segregated girls. No attempt was ever made to record the preference of the whole intake to mixed or single sex setting, but casual conversations and occasional spontaneous discussion in Maths lessons generally revealed that single sex sets were popular with a clear majority of girls. Nevertheless, there were many girls who believed that mixed sets would have been preferable.

Some of the girls who believed they preferred Maths without boys commented that segregation created a more serious working environment.

Angela: 'I think it's better. We act daft with boys around. I think I've done better in Maths than I would have done. I think girls on their own, it gets more serious.'

Maureen: 'Well, you sort of settle down quicker, no boys messing about, and you can talk more freely with the teacher without having boys about, and when you answer, the girls are OK, but boys laugh at you.'

Maureen was not the only girl concerned about the boys laughing at her.

Jennifer: 'Yes, it's better. Because the lads, they put you down. If you get anything wrong, they laugh and say "You should have got that." And with all the girls, you sort of get on better.'

The interviews with the mixed intake suggested that some girls (such as Audrey) were so self-conscious of the boys that their performance in Maths had been hindered. One girl at least from the segregated intake was similarly embarrassed by boys.

Karen: 'Well, if we were mixed, I'd be in a lower set. And I'd be really embarrassed with boys around. When the test marks are read out, I'd be petrified in case I was near the bottom.'

> 'It's freer in a girls' set. You can speak more freely. I'd always be wondering what I looked like, if my hair was sticking up (giggle). I'm much more relaxed with girls.'

Despite the perceived advantages of segregation to this group of girls, there was general agreement that single sex sets should not be expanded to other subjects.

Jennifer: 'They (the boys) just sit there as though they're the best. It puts you off. But I don't really mind in the other subjects. I just keep my concentration.'

Maureen: 'Well, I suppose in English, I seem to get on better. I'm more sure of myself.'

The girls who would have preferred mixed Maths sets felt that the presence of boys created a livelier and more competitive atmosphere in lessons.

Sarah: 'Well, it's quieter (in Maths), there's no joking like with the boys. It's livelier somehow (with boys). The girls are competing with the lads, but it breaks up the lesson, and things go better somehow.'

Christine: I prefer mixed, because you find lads, they sort of break the ice, the girls can be dead bitchy with each other, can't they? And I've got to do this, and I've got to do that, but lads, they soon break the ice. They take everything in their stride.'

Conclusions

A handful of interviews, such as those conducted with the girls of both intakes, cannot go very far in untangling the complexity of factors which cause so many secondary schoolgirls to under-achieve in Maths, and come to regard Maths as a very difficult subject. Nevertheless, the interviews did provide some interesting pointers.

The great majority of girls of both intakes believed that the onset of their difficulties in Maths came in the middle three years of secondary education, and this was generally associated with an ability to cope with the speed at which they were expected to move from topic to topic. Several girls expressed the need to go over difficult points again and again until comprehension was achieved.

Several of the interviews with the mixed intake did suggest that some of the girls at least had suffered from the presence of boys in Maths lessons, and none of the mixed girls could suggest the positive benefits of mixed Maths classes: indeed, there was apparently very little or no positive communication between boys and girls in Maths classes.

The girls of the segregated intake generally agreed that the atmosphere in their Maths classes was quiet and serious. This was appreciated by those girls who were bothered by the presence and behaviour of boys in mixed classes, but other girls, who were not intimidated by boys, would have preferred a lively, competitive atmosphere which they felt mixed Maths classes provided.

Finally, the Maths teachers were generally highly regarded by the girls of both intakes. Help was readily available for the girls whether they were in mixed or segregated sets. Most teachers were considered to be supportive.

These opinions are valuable, for the Maths teachers as a group have been very concerned about the general performance of girls in Maths for many years. It is a matter of policy at the school that every effort should be made to encourage the girls whether they are taught in mixed or segregated sets, and each Maths teacher is conscious of the need to involve girls actively in the lessons. Furthermore, the majority of Maths teachers is female and there is a strong commitment to this work. Perhaps the most significant point to emerge from these interviews is that despite this strong commitment to equal opportunity for girls in Maths, some of the girls from the mixed intake still seem to have been handicapped by the presence of boys in Maths lessons. This poses an important question. What is happening to girls in Maths lessons in those mixed schools which have not yet given thought to equality of opportunity?

8 The teachers' views

The interviews

Interviews were held with six full-time Maths teachers, (four female, two male) who had been on the staff of the school when single sex setting in Maths was introduced, all of whom had acquired considerable experience of teaching both segregated and mixed sets by the winter of 1985 when the interviews took place. The only two-full time Maths teachers not to be interviewed were the head of department (male), who was a new appointment in September 1982, and the remedial specialist (female) most of whose pupils were not included in this investigation.

The teachers' comments were inevitably highly subjective being based on personal experiences with individual sets. Nevertheless there was a considerable unanimity of opinion on many of the points raised in the interviews.

Single sex setting

When single sex setting had been discussed in department meetings in the late 1970s, despite the general concern about the under-achievement of so many girls, several teachers had been sceptical about the potential benefits of segregated sets. Furthermore concern was expressed about forming segregated Maths sets from pupils who had opted to attend a mixed school. By 1985 most of these doubts had disappeared.

Female Teacher: 'I suppose some people would argue that boys and girls have to compete when they leave school, so they should be mixed for Maths. But all we're trying to do is enable them to cope and gain more confidence. It's like anything else. There's no point in sticking to a rigid system if it isn't working well. We had to do something about it to help the girls.'

Male Teacher: 'In 1980, I was very much against the idea (of single sex setting), but I was largely looking at it from my point of view, but for reasons I've mentioned before, I do think the girls have benefited from it, certainly the two sets I've taught, there's been greater participation from girls than had boys been present.'

Female Teacher: 'In a lot more cases than I expected, there has been some benefit. Not just girls. When I think of my second year boys' group last year, I think some of those boys benefited being on their own.'

Some of the teachers felt that some boys had gained from segregated Maths lessons, but the others felt that segregation had not really affected the boys at all. All six teachers however believed that girls had gained more from single sex setting than boys.

Female Teacher: 'Girls benefit most from single setting. It gives them confidence. The boys don't seem to miss out. Hopefully, the results will show the girls doing better. When I think a few years ago, there were only four girls in the top Maths set. We've come a long way since then. The gap between boys and girls has dropped enormously.'

Male Teacher: 'I think girls do benefit from it in that they tend to get more confident, mainly the fact that they are all together, they're more confident as a social group and therefore it comes through in their work. I know we try to involve everyone, but you find that girls will not offer comments or answers when the boys are there.'

Female Teacher: 'I think that girls on the whole benefit more from single sex setting. Just thinking back to the classes I've had, I would say, yes, the girls I have at the moment, a third year set (of girls), who need, despite the fact they're the top set, they need a couple of explanations on most points. And on the third explanation, perhaps most of them will have understood it! And I don't think they mind. I feel there's more contact between me as a teacher and them as pupils because they're not afraid to say "I don't know what your'e talking about", or "I don't understand that". And I feel they're more inclined to say that than if there are boys present.'

The popularity of single sex sets for Maths with the majority of boys and girls was recognised by most of the teachers.

Female Teacher: 'Most of the children like to work in single sex sets. It's very popular, even the fifth year. I have a boys' set this year. They're happier as a boys' set. They don't want to be mixed with the girls for Maths.'

Female Teacher: 'I think the girls are in favour of being on their own; indeed, they've told me they prefer being on their own.'

First and second years

All six teachers felt that single sex setting was of much greater value in Lower School (first and second years) than in Upper School (third, fourth and fifth years).

Female Teacher: 'I like single setting in Lower School. I really do. I think it's smashing there. Both girls on their own and boys on their own. You can really get to grips with a class, you can develop a relationship which works. I wouldn't want to go back to mixed sets lower down the school.'

Female Teacher: 'I think to the majority of children, single sex sets are better (surprisingly) early on than further up the school. I think the first year children – particularly the girls – appreciate not having to put up with boys who, at that point, can be an annoyance, and I think they appreciate being able to get on with it without them prodding and poking and making rude comments.'

One teacher described how first year boys and girls differed in their approach to a particular lesson. This example provides support to the view that 11 and 12 year old girls are both less interested and less competent in practical work than boys.

Male Teacher: 'We did practical work with a first year all boys set and then an all girls set. Same ability. It was practical work on measuring. We did the estimations in class, we talked about estimating, and the attitude then was the boys were really, really keen and wanted to get out and measure and when they went out to measure, they were very, very accurate and worked extremely hard. They wanted to make sure their results were right. They did the exercise, and then checked their work. The estimations and measurements of the two sets were similar, but the way the girls worked when they had to go out, they did not have the same attitude. They weren't enthusisastic, and their approach was very haphazard, they would put the tape measure down and squabble as to who should hold it. Then someone would walk off with it. They didn't seem to be able to organise themselves.

A rough guide or estimate was good enough. Most of them were not prepared to measure carefully and check their answers. They lacked the willingness to ensure the work was right and accurate.'

Fine setting

One serious disadvantage of single sex setting was that it prevented fine setting (the practice of placing pupils in sets where they are very closely matched by ability). This did not matter in the first and second years, because the pupils were traditionally placed in broad ability bands for Maths at this stage, and this was still possible with single sex sets. When it came to exam work in the fourth and fifth years, however, the teachers felt it important that the most able boys and girls in particular should be combined in a mixed set.

Female Teacher: 'The very top end feel they would have been happier with the opposite sex because there would have been closer setting – there would not have been such a wide ability range. They say quite a lot – at time the brighter girls and boys have been very bored because the teacher has had to go over particular points again and again. At that ability level there is no question of them being bothered by the presence of the opposite sex, they would revel in the competition. Even the shyest girl in the top set – who is very capable – would have preferred mixing for Maths.'

Discipline problems

Four of the teachers interviewed believed that single sex setting had created discipline problems in some Maths lessons with the older pupils. These problems were most serious in the lower ability boys' sets, but the girls sets too were sometimes difficult to teach. These four teachers believed that among older pupils, mixed sets were better behaved.

Female Teacher: 'I think we have created discipline problems at the top end of the school – the older pupils. There isn't the flexibility to separate Bill Bloggs from Joe Soap as you would have been able to with mixed sets. It's not only the boys' sets, some of the girls' sets are very difficult, in the upper age bracket, and I think this is because they're separated.

The fourth year boys' set I had last year are very hard to teach. I do feel that if they had been leavened with some girls, they wouldn't have been quite so difficult, and some of the behaviour wouldn't have taken place, because they wouldn't have done the sort of thing they were doing in front of girls. They would have lost face.'

Male Teacher: 'I think that with low ability boys, the discipline problems are immense. One third year boys set I had were particularly bad, there were many discipline problems and motivation was very difficult. They didn't have the concentration, and nothing seems to settle them.

Mixing the sets does have a settling effect, because even the girls when they're together (pause) they tend to set each other off. When they're mixed, they wouldn't say some of the things they say in a single sex group.'

One teacher, however, strongly disagreed with these views about discipline.

Female Teacher: 'I personally think that discipline is better in single sex sets – they're far too easily distracted, sort of not by the amount of work they're doing or the type of work they're doing, but by the distractions that have nothing to do with the work. The fifth year group I took last year – a mixed group – I'd had some of those boys and girls for three years and I felt that some of the girls would have benefited from not being with boys. They would have settled and concentrated more on their own.'

Summarising teachers' views

The teachers were asked whether they were generally in favour or against single sex setting in Maths. All six had mixed opinions and were unable to give a simple positive or negative reply. They felt that many individual pupils had benefited from single sex setting, and this was particularly noticeable among first and second year girls. Nevertheless, they all recognised that segregating the sexes for Maths had also created problems.

Female Teacher: 'Summing up; it isn't simple to judge single sex setting. It's not black and white. It's a beautiful collection of shades of grey.'

9 Conclusions

Improved female Maths performance

No proper evaluation of the effects of segregating the school intake of 1980 for Maths lessons can be made until consideration is given to the general improvement in the performance of girls in Maths in recent years. An attempt has been made to illustrate this point in Table 9.1 which details the 'O' level Maths passes of boys and girls since the school was created in its present form in September 1970.

Table 9.1 GCE 'O' Level passes in Maths, by sex [1]

Year of examination	Boy passes	Girl passes
1971	Precise details	Precise details
1972	not available	not available
1973	but between 20	but not more than
1974	and 30 boys passed	two girls passed
1975	every year between	in any year between
1976	1971 and 1976	1971 and 1976
1977	24	1
1978	13	2
1979	24	9
1980	25	1
1981	28	13
1982	29	9
1983	28	15
1984	22[2]	15[2]
1985	28[2]	23[2]

[1] GCE 'O' level grades 'A', 'B' or 'C' or CSE grade 1.
[2] The numbers shown here are greater than those shown in Table 6.2 because they include many pupils excluded from the investigation (e.g. high ability pupils, non-counters from Table 1 and late-comers to the school). They show the girls' results in rather better light than Table 6.2. This is because in both intakes there were rather more able girls than able boys excluded from the investigation.

In every year from 1971 to 1978 there were never more than two girls who passed 'O' level Maths, but in recent years there has been a dramatic improvement. It should be noted that this improvement has taken place both with girls who have been taught in mixed sets and girls who have been taught in segregated sets (including girls from the pilot experiment of 1978–80 who sat 'O' levels in 1983).

It is particularly pleasing that this improvement in the girls' results has apparently not been made at the expense of the boys, for the boys' Maths passes have remained remarkably stable (with the sole exception of 1978) throughout the 15-year period.

There has of course been some national improvement in the performance of girls taking 'O' Level Maths over the same period. The EOC statistical profile 'Women and Men in Britain' (1985) reveals that whereas girls made up only 37·5% of successful candidates in 1970, they made up 43·6% of the total in 1983. Nevertheless, it would appear that the changing image of Maths at the school has also contributed to the improvement in the girls' results there. There is no doubt that most of the girls at the school (whether they have been taught in mixed sets or segregated sets) no longer regard Maths as a predominantly masculine subject.

Commitment of the school

One important factor was the recruitment of three female Maths teachers in the late 1970's which has meant that in recent years over half of Maths lessons have been taught by women. The sustained efforts made by all Maths teachers at the school to ensure that girls play an active part in class (whether the sets have been mixed or segregated) must also have had a beneficial effect. Additionally, attempts to change the male bias of the syllabus have borne fruit. In recent years, the improving performance of many girls has resulted in an increased ratio of girls to boys in the top mixed Maths sets. Consequently, these girls in the top sets have not had to endure the isolation of their predecessors in the 1970's.

These points all seem to suggest that a school which mounts a sustained and coherent campaign to provide equal opportunities for girls in Maths classes can succeed without using the particular device of single sex setting; indeed, some of the statistical results of this investigation suggest that in this particular school, single sex setting has had a negligible effect, at least with the older girls. In the four short tests and the external examinations, the differences in performance between mixed boys and segregated boys and between mixed girls and segregated girls were not significant. The two groups of boys displayed very similar attitudes to Maths and, with the sole exception of the utility scale, the same was true of the two groups of girls.

The majority of the fifth year girls from the mixed intake who were interviewed were certainly critical of the behaviour of the boys in Maths, but the results of this investigation suggest that most girls are resilient enough to overcome any problems created by such behaviour. The practice of the girls in working together in pairs or in small groups, coupled with the ready support and assistance of the teachers has apparently enabled most girls to cope perfectly well in mixed Maths classes.

Remaining problems

Despite the progress which has been made by the girls, however, it would be quite wrong for the school to be complacent at this stage, for when the pupils were matched by ability, the performance of the fourth and fifth year girls in Maths still fell short of parity with the boys whether the girls had been taught in mixed or in segregated sets.

Furthermore, fourth year girls, whether they had been taught in mixed or segregated sets, pereceived Maths as a significantly more difficult subject than did boys. Although this difference was consistent with the findings of the second and third APU Secondary Surveys (1981 and 1982), and although the perception of the difficulty of Maths does not appear to be closely related to performance, it is a matter of concern that many capable girls are presumably discouraged from studying Maths beyond the age of 16 because they regard the subject as difficult.

Additionally, it would appear from the interviews with the fifth year girls that a small minority of girls have been inhibited by the presence of boys in Maths classes to the extent that performance in Maths may have been affected. It would be wrong to ignore the interests of such girls.

The belief of all teachers at the school with a wide experience of teaching Maths to single sex sets that segregated sets were particularly helpful to first and second year girls is clearly important. This belief is supported not only by the results of the pilot experiment of 1978–80 (which covered just the first and second years) but also by the results of the Tameside Numeracy Test (taken part way through the third year) which indicated that segregated girls performed significantly better than mixed girls on six of the 13 topics covered.

The problem would seem to be that the gains made by segregated girls in the first and second years have not been maintained, for both the girls from the pilot experiment (who were placed in mixed Maths sets from the third year) and the segregated girls in this investigation (who remained in segregated sets) eventually performed no better than the mixed girls they had been matched with in the external examinations.

Implications

If single sex sets in Maths are to be retained at the school in the first and second years, serious thought should be given to the possibility of developing a separate scheme of work to meet the special needs of girls at this formative stage of their secondary education.

It would be inappropriate for this report to be dogmatic about the form which any separate scheme of work for girls should take, but certain guidelines can be suggested.

For instance, the practical tests included in the two APU Primary Surveys (1978 and 1979) and in the three APU Secondary Surveys (1980, 1981 and 1982) all included many items in which the boys performed significantly better than the girls and this indicates that practical Maths should be an important element in any separate scheme of work. This particular need was highlighted by the example of the male Maths teacher at the school who noted the superior performance of the first year boys' set over the girls' set on a practical exercise concerned with estimation and measurement.

Secondly, there are many Maths topics in which girls apparently need particular assistance. For instance, in the responses which the mixed and segregated intakes of the school made to the APU Mathematics Attitude Questionnaire, it was noted that both mixed girls and segregated girls regarded scale problems and geometrical constructions as significantly more difficult than the two groups of boys. Other Maths topics which girls find significantly more difficult than boys are mentioned in the APU Primary and Secondary Surveys and by Ward in Schools Council Working Paper No. 61 (1979).

Finally, this investigation does point to the conclusion that girls generally need to spend more time than boys in developing problem-solving skills. In the four short tests, which contained a high proportion of items requiring problem-solving skills, the two groups of boys performed significantly better than both the mixed girls and segregated girls. This conclusion is also supported by the results of other more comprehensive pieces of research. In a review of a number of American studies dealing with pupils aged ten to fourteen, Fennema (1974) concluded that boys performed significantly better than girls in 54 out of 77 Maths tests involving complex, cognitive skills (comprehension, application and analysis), and Wood in his analysis of the responses to 1973 and 1974 'O' Level Maths papers (1976) concluded that 'none of the items on which girls out-performed boys required what could be termed problem-solving behaviour.'

It is of course recognised that there is nothing particularly novel in the guidelines for a separate scheme of work for girls suggested here. After all, the Cockcroft Report 'Mathematics Counts' (1982) stated that for all pupils computational skills should be related to practical situations and applied to problems, and there is no doubt that the Maths Department at Stamford High School is already attempting to apply the major recommendations of this report.

It is also important to recognise the recent research of Walden and Walkerdine (1985) which suggests that the performance of girls in Maths does not decline as they progress through secondary school. In a fourth year secondary test which they analysed, the girls consistently out-performed the boys. Many secondary Maths teachers however frequently equate good learning with 'flair' and such masculine traits as rule challenging and outspokenness and they have less regard for the quiet, hard-working and conformist approach displayed by many girls. In consequence, girls are less likely to be stretched and challenged than boys and they are also less likely to be entered for 'O' level Maths. Many girls find themselves caught up in a struggle to discover a way of behaving and learning which satisfies their need to be feminine, but which also shows the qualities which are equated with classroom success. In the face of such conflict, many special strategies to improve the attainment of girls in Maths may actually prove to be counter-productive.

This is not the place to discuss Walden and Walkerdine's complex research in detail, but the evidence produced by this investigation does suggest that at Stamford High School at least, many able fourth year girls are still under-achieving in Maths, and it is therefore appropriate to recommend remedial action. It is felt that a special scheme of work in Maths, designed to stimulate the interest and imagination of 11 and 12 year old girls taught in segregated sets could not only improve attainment but also help these girls to form positive attitudes towards the subject. A sound foundation in the first and second years could eventually lead to parity of performance with the boys in external examinations.

APPENDIX I
The Organisation of Maths at Stamford High School

Throughout the six academic years of this investigation (September 1979–July 1985), the main establishment of the Maths Department was as follows:

1. Head of Department (male)
1. 2nd in Department (female)
2. Male teachers (one of whom spent one year on secondment)
3. Female teachers (one of whom for some years had a light teaching load because of her responsibilities as Head of Lower School, and another of whom for some years taught a combination of Maths and Science)
1. Remedial specialist (female)

All of these teachers were experienced and fully qualified Maths teachers. The Head of Department retired in July 1982 and was replaced by an outside appointment. The remainder of this group remained on the strength of the school throughout the period of the investigation.

The balance of Maths teaching on the timetable was taken by teachers who taught Maths in combination with other subjects or responsibilities. The constitution of this group differed from year to year, but all the teachers who were used in this way were both experienced and qualified Maths teachers. They included, for instance, two male Deputy Head teachers and a female teacher of some 20 years experience who taught Maths together with PE and Games. Most of the teachers in this second group were male, and this helped to redress the numerical superiority of female teachers in the first group.

Meetings of the Maths Department are held at frequent intervals to discuss such matters as the sequence of mathematical topics to be dealt with by each year group, and the setting of tests and internal examinations. Additional meetings are held from time to time to discuss classroom problems, teaching methods and alternative approaches to different topics on the syllabus. Proposed revisions and amendments to the syllabus are also discussed at such meetings.

In fact, no major revisions to the Maths syllabus were made during the period of this investigation. The current syllabus covers a very broad spectrum of Maths including a wide range of both 'traditional' and 'modern' topics (although this division is perhaps not appropriate nowadays). Ability setting of one form or another is applied to all year groups, and an attempt is made to introduce most topics on the syllabus to all sets (although the more able sets obviously deal with each topic in greater depth). Remedial sets and non-exam sets in the fourth and fifth years however do spend a greater proportion of time on 'everyday' Maths than on more academic topics. An element of practical work, related to topics currently being dealt with in class, is included for all sets in every term. A certain amount of individual and group work is attempted with remedial and non-exam sets (which are small in size), but teaching methods are generally traditional throughout the Maths Department.

Both the mixed intake and the segregated intake spent the first three weeks of the first year in mixed ability sets before taking an initial Maths test. (This test was amended between 1979 and 1980 and the results could therefore not be used for comparing the two intakes). After this test, the mixed intake was divided for Maths into two half year groups each comprising two 'A' sets, two 'B' sets and a (smaller) remedial set. The segregated intake was divided into five boys' sets and give girls' sets each comprising two 'A' sets, two 'B' sets and a remedial set.

These setting arrangements continued for both intakes until the end of the second year. In the third year, both intakes were again organised into two groups of five Maths sets, but this time the groups were all set finely by ability.

In the fourth year, the mixed intake was divided into ten Maths sets according to ability, the majority of pupils being placed in sets preparing for external examinations. This setting arrangement was followed until the pupils left school. The segregated intake remained in separate boys' and girls' sets in the fourth and fifth years, with the sets containing the more able pupils preparing for external examinations.

The set sizes of both intakes were similar throughout the five years, although they did vary slightly from time to time with promotions and demotions, pupils moving to other schools, and new pupils arriving. The similarity in the size of sets is illustrated below:

Mean size of Maths sets (excluding remedial sets) at the beginning of the third year:

Mixed Intake   26.1

Segregated Boys   25.0
Segregated Girls   26.0

The mixed intake and the segregated intake were allocated an equal amount of time for Maths on the timetable as follows:

1st Year } 3 lessons of 70 minutes per week
2nd Year }

3rd Year   2 lessons of 70 minutes and 1 lesson of 35 minutes per week

4th Year } 3 lessons of 70 minutes per week
5th Year }

Finally, when the Maths timetable is constructed, the school follows a policy of combining the best teams of teachers available for each year group irrespective of the sex of each teacher, and this policy was followed for the segregated intake. In other words, no attempt was made to place the girls' sets exclusively with female teachers and the boys' sets exclusively with male teachers. However, two teachers (one male, one female) did express a preference for teaching pupils of their own sex whenever possible and this factor was taken into account. Consequently the segregated girls did spend a higher proportion of their time in Maths with female teachers than did mixed girls and similarly the segregated boys did spend a higher porportion of their time in Maths with male teachers than did mixed boys. This point is illustrated below:

Percentage of Maths lessons spent by each group of pupils with male and female teachers throughout the period of the investigation

	Female Teachers	Male Teachers
Mixed boys	54	46
Segregated boys	49	51
Mixed girls	52	48
Segregated girls	61	39
Mixed intake (combined)	53	47
Segregated intake (combined)	55	45

APPENDIX II
Statistical methods and Significance Tests

Box and Whisker Plots

The sets of scores achieved by each group of pupils in the following tests are displayed in the form of 'box and whisker plots' in later appendices to this report:

    Non-Verbal Test DH (Appendix III)
    Tameside Numeracy Test (Appendix IV)
    Four Short-Tests (Appendix V)
    APU Mathematics Attitude Questionnaire (Appendix VI)

In each case, four 'box and whisker plots' (one for each group of pupils) are displayed side by side so that visual comparisons between the performance of the different groups can be made quite easily.

The following illustration indicates the information available from each plot:

Title of test (full score range of test)

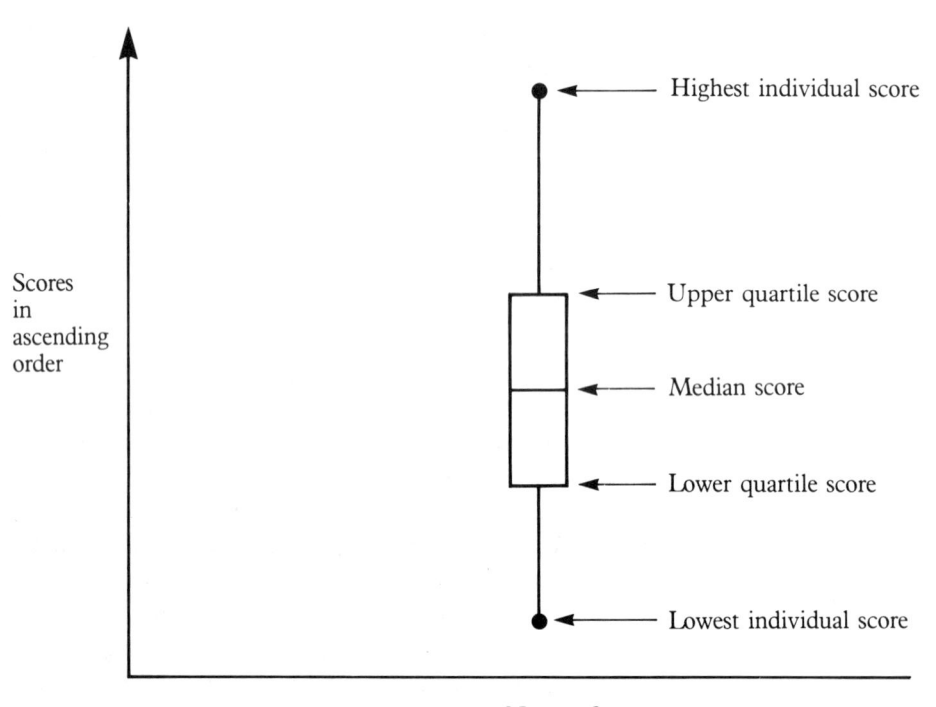

Scores in ascending order

- Highest individual score
- Upper quartile score
- Median score
- Lower quartile score
- Lowest individual score

Name of group
Number in group
Mean score

Significance

Throughout this Report the terms 'significant' and 'statistically significant' mean that the probability of the differences between the two sets of scores being compared having occurred by chance is 5% or less, and the term 'highly significant' means that the probability of such differences occurring by chance is 1% or less.

Significance tests

In all cases throughout this investigation, the significance tests used were two-tailed.

The decision to match pupils by ability for this investigation led to the conclusion that if possible a paired t test (Guilford and Fruchter 1981, pp 152–155) should be used to compare the paired scores of the different groups of pupils on the following:

Tameside Numeracy Test (total scores)

Four Short-Tests (combined scores)

Difficulty Score ⎫
Utility Score ⎬ APU Maths Attitude Questionnaire
Enjoyment Score ⎭

As the paired t test is a parametric test, its use is dependent on the sets of scores to be compared conforming fairly closely to the normal curve of distribution. Consequently the sets of scores achieved by each one of the four groups of pupils referred to in the paragraph above was subjected to Geary's Test (Burroughs 1971 pp 194–5). Geary's Test revealed that although most of these sets of scores did not differ significantly from normality, a few of them were not suitable for parametric testing.

Bearing in mind that the number of scores in each set to be tested was above 60, the Wilcoxon Matched-Pairs Signed-Ranks Test (Siegel 1956 pp 75–83) was selected as the most suitable non-parametric alternative to the paired t test.

In the event, these sets of scores were compared by using both the paired t test and the Wilcoxon Test, and the significance scores which were produced by the two tests were very similar. This report uses the significance scores produced by the Wilcoxon Test.

When it came to comparing the performance of the four groups of pupils on the individual topics of the Tameside Numeracy Test, and on each individual one of the Four Short Tests, a different procedure was adopted, for in both these cases the significance test was to be applied on an item by item basis (that is, by comparing the number of pupils in each group who answered each item correctly). Many of the sets of numbers to be compared differed significantly from the normal curve of distribution and consequently non-parametric testing was appropriate. Two separate tests were selected for this group of comparisons as follows:

Where the number of items to be tested did not exceed ten	The Randomization Test for Matched Pairs (Siegel 1956, pp 88–91)
Where the number of items to be tested did exceed ten	The Wilcoxon Matched-Pairs Signed-Ranks Test.

Finally, the chi-square significance test was used to compare both the external examination results of the four groups of pupils and the responses of these groups to individual statements on the Mathematics Attitude Questionnaire. With some of these statements, the number of cells containing fewer than five responses exceeded 20% of the total and this placed a limitation on the use of the chi-square test. Where this was the case, the 'agree' and 'strongly agree' cells and the 'disagree' and 'strongly disagree' cells were combined to increase the number of responses in each cell. On some occasions, these amalgamations still failed to reduce sufficiently the number of cells with fewer than five responses. In these cases, the significance scores produced were not considered valid whenever the small cells had a material influence on the outcome.

APPENDIX III

NFER non-verbal test DH: Analysis

DISTRIBUTION OF SCORES BY GROUP (RANGE 70–140)

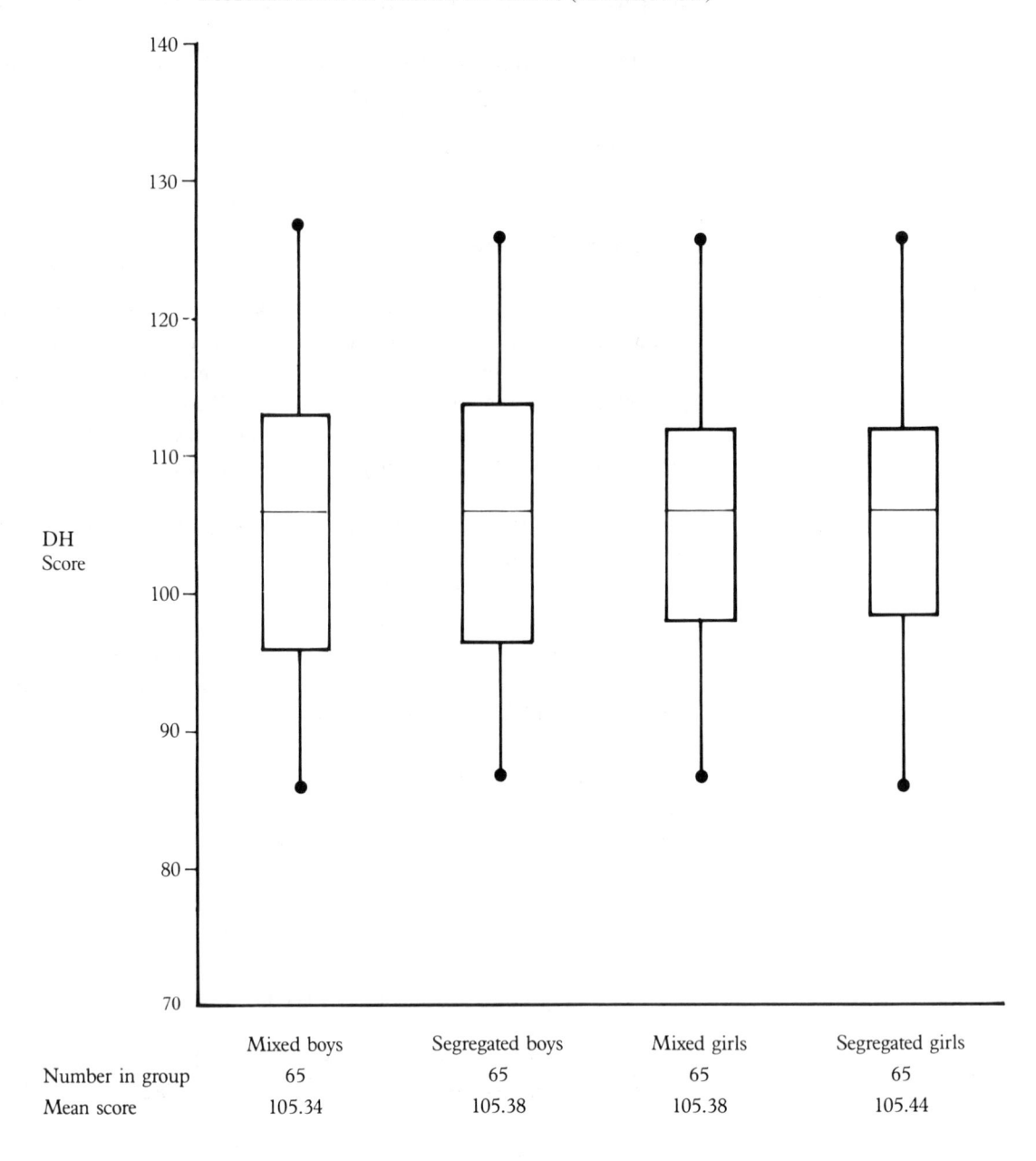

	Mixed boys	Segregated boys	Mixed girls	Segregated girls
Number in group	65	65	65	65
Mean score	105.34	105.38	105.38	105.44

APPENDIX IV
Tameside Numeracy Test: Analysis

(a) DISTRIBUTION OF SCORES BY GROUP (RANGE 0–112)

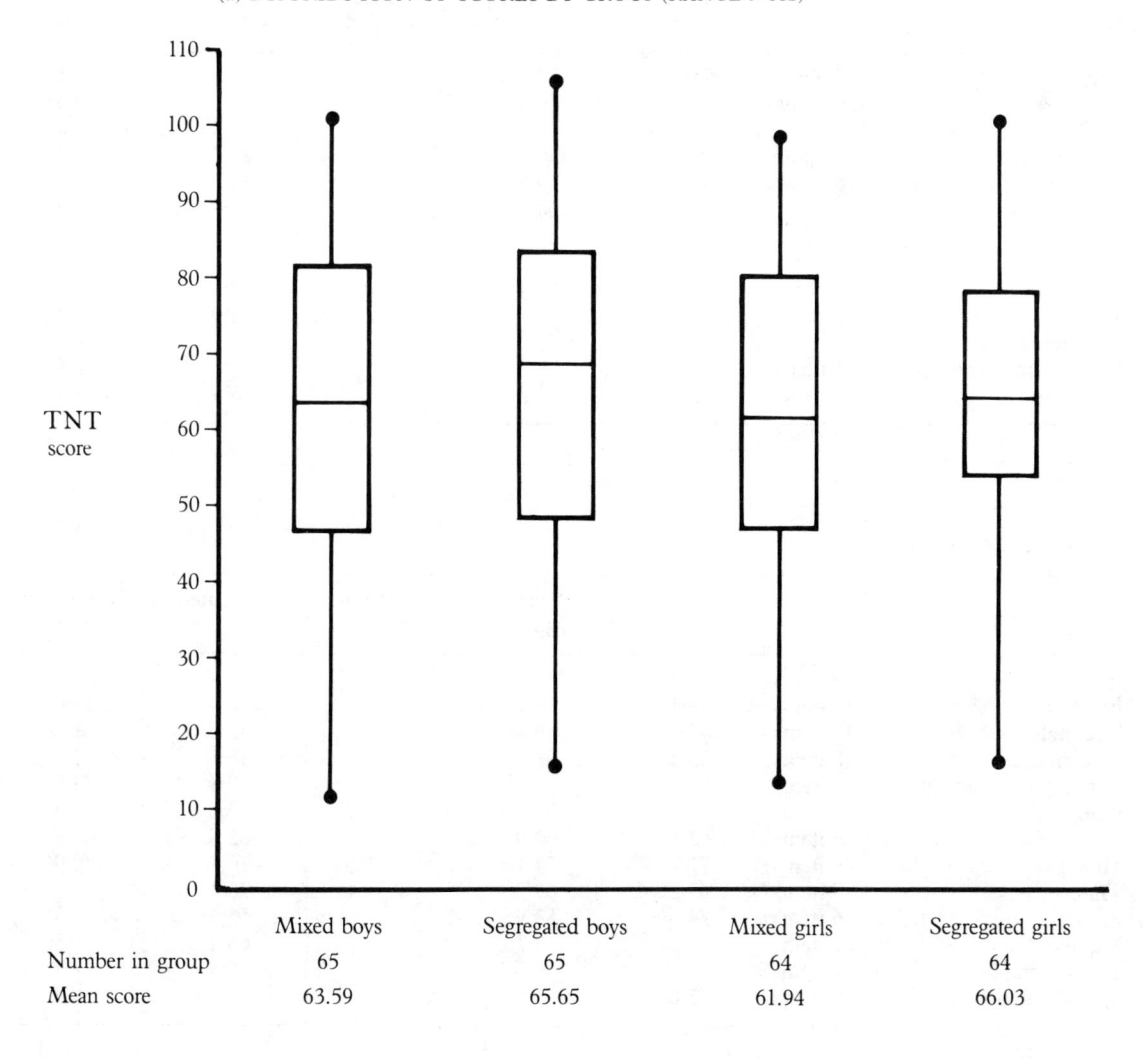

	Mixed boys	Segregated boys	Mixed girls	Segregated girls
Number in group	65	65	64	64
Mean score	63.59	65.65	61.94	66.03

(b) MEAN SCORES BY TOPIC

Mixed compared with segregated pupils   *percentages*

Topic		Mixed boys	Segregated boys	Significant difference	Mixed girls	Segregated girls	Significant difference
Integers	(19 items)	75·2	77·4		74·3	76·1	
Fractions	(19 items)	38·3	40·4		36·7	39·6	★
Decimals	(15 items)	40·7	42·6		39·4	44·0	★
Percentages	(8 items)	33·5	36·5		31·0	32·5	
Volume and Capacity	(6 items)	68·7	70·8		63·0	73·8	★
Length	(6 items)	60·5	60·0		52·6	57·9	
Mass	(5 items)	62·8	62·8		60·0	65·3	
Money	(5 items)	71·7	70·2		74·1	80·0	★
Time	(7 items)	69·2	70·1		69·9	74·5	★
Area	(6 items)	54·6	55·6		53·9	53·3	
Number	(5 items)	70·2	66·1		69·7	77·5	★
Tables, graphs and charts	(6 items)	73·9	78·4		79·7	77·7	
Spatial relationships	(5 items)	52·0	65·2	★	50·9	56·9	★

Boys compared with girls

Topic		Mixed boys	Mixed girls	Significant difference	Segregated boys	Segregated girls	Significant difference
Integers	(19 items)	75·2	74·3		77·4	76·1	
Fractions	(19 items)	38·3	36·7		40·4	39·6	
Decimals	(15 items)	40·7	39·4		42·6	44·0	
Percentages	(8 items)	33·5	31·0		36·5	32·5	
Volume and Capacity	(6 items)	68·7	63·0		70·8	73·8	
Length	(6 items)	60·5	52·6		60·0	57·9	
Mass	(5 items)	62·8	60·0		62·8	65·3	
Money	(5 items)	71·7	74·1		70·2	80·0	★
Time	(7 items)	69·2	69·9		70·1	74·5	
Area	(6 items)	54·6	53·9		55·6	53·3	
Number	(5 items)	70·2	69·7		66·1	77·5	★
Tables, graphs and charts	(6 items)	73·9	79·7		78·4	77·7	
Spatial relationships	(5 items)	52·0	50·9		65·2	56·9	

★ The difference is significant at the 5% level.

APPENDIX V
Four Short Tests: Analysis

(a) DISTRIBUTION OF SCORES BY GROUP (RANGE 0–43)

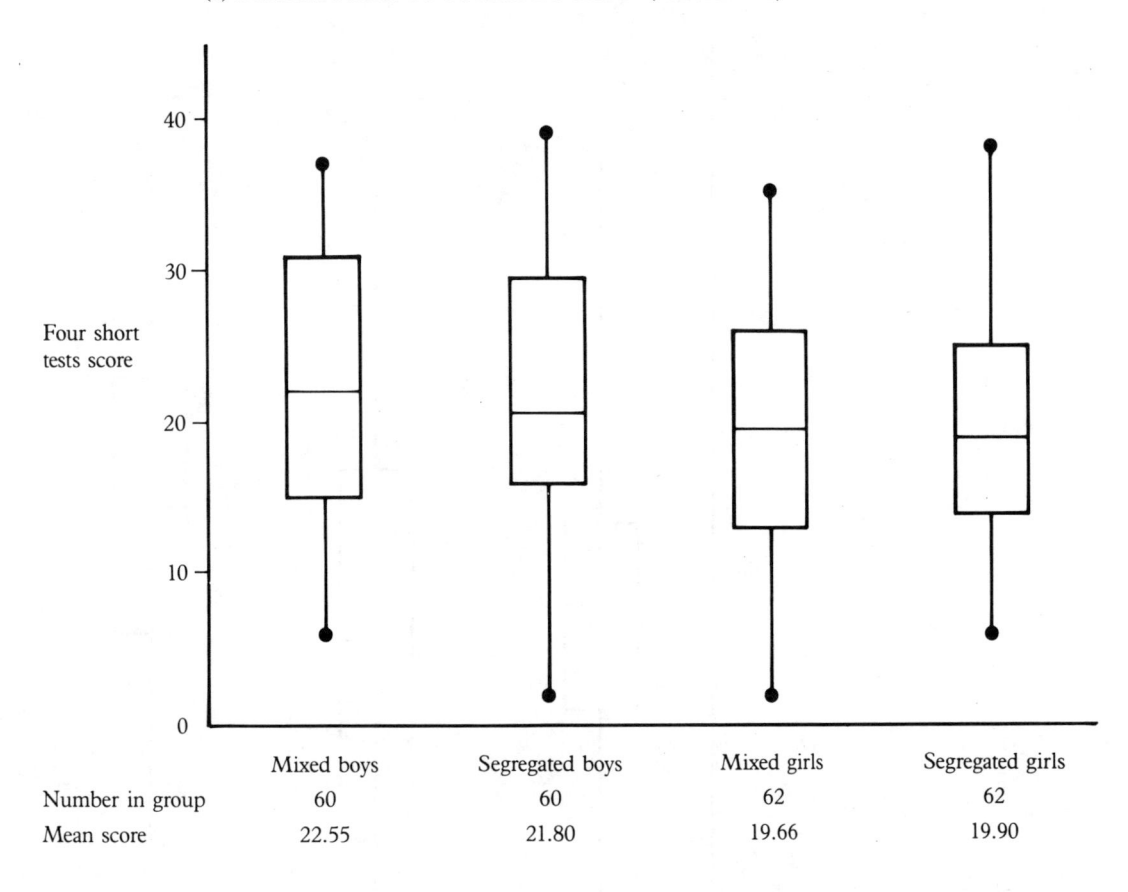

	Mixed boys	Segregated boys	Mixed girls	Segregated girls
Number in group	60	60	62	62
Mean score	22.55	21.80	19.66	19.90

(b) MEAN SCORES BY TEST

Mixed compared with segregated pupils *percentages*

Test		Mixed boys	Segregated boys	Significant difference	Mixed girls	Segregated girls	Significant difference
Test 1 (Geometry)	13 items	56·3	55·4		46·9	48·8	
Test 2 (Proportion, rates, ratio)	8 items	56·3	49·0	*	49·4	44·1	
Test 3 (Mensuration)	8 items	43·5	40·4		31·0	34·6	
Test 4 (Algebra)	14 items	51·8	53·2		50·9	51·7	

Boys compared with girls

Test		Mixed boys	Mixed girls	Significant difference	Segregated boys	Segregated girls	Significant difference
Test 1 (Geometry)	13 items	56·3	46·9	**	55·4	48·8	*
Test 2 (Proportion, rates, ratio)	8 items	56·3	49·4	*	49·0	44·1	
Test 3 (Mensuration)	8 items	43·5	31·0	**	40·4	34·6	
Test 4 (Algebra)	14 items	51·8	50·9		53·2	51·7	

* The difference is significant at the 5% level.
** The difference is significant at the 1% level.

APPENDIX VI
APU Maths attitude Questionnaire: Analysis

(a) DIFFICULTY SCALE (RANGE 17–85). DISTRIBUTION OF SCORES BY GROUP

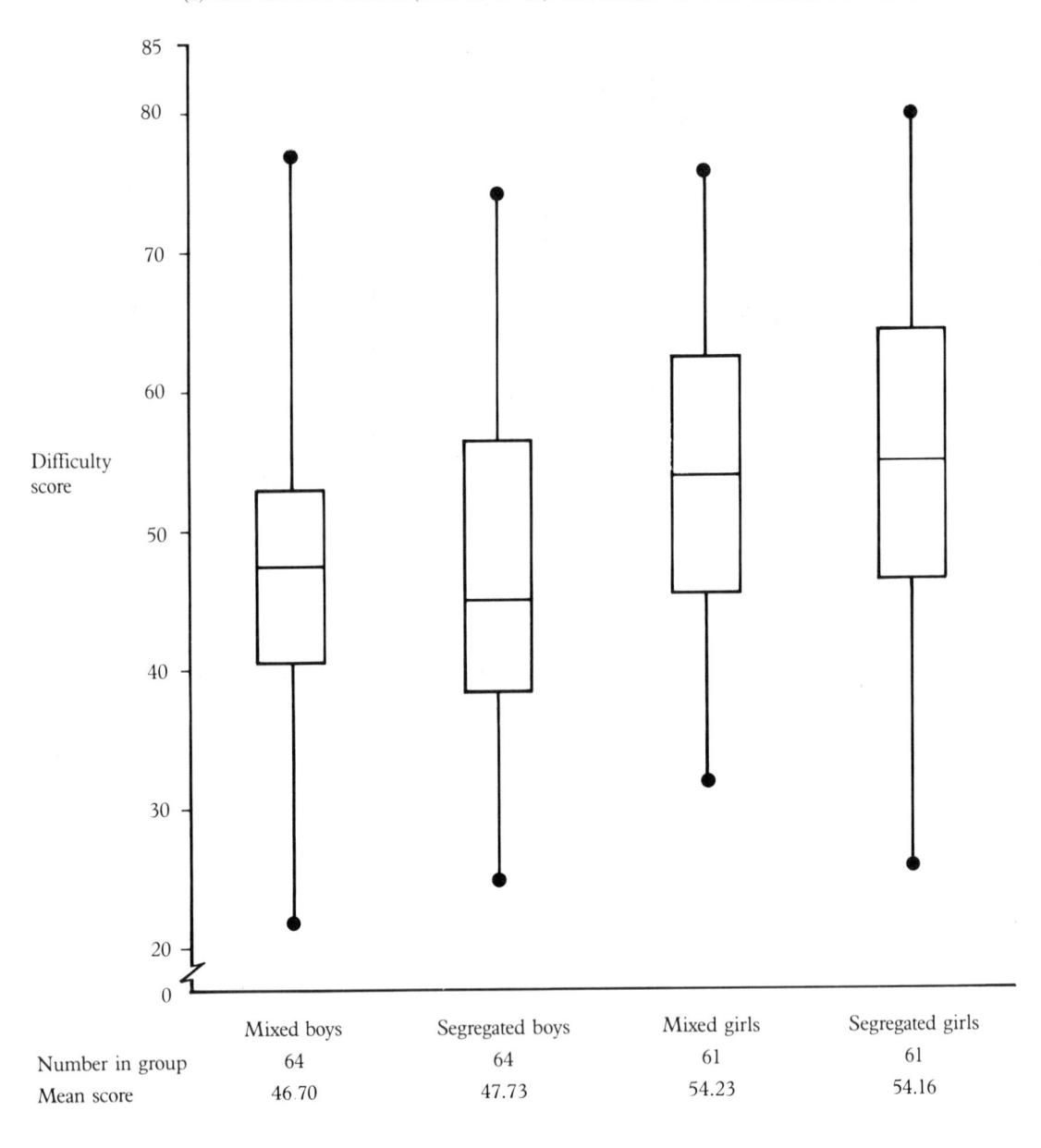

	Mixed boys	Segregated boys	Mixed girls	Segregated girls
Number in group	64	64	61	61
Mean score	46.70	47.73	54.23	54.16

(b) TOPICS RANKED IN PERCEIVED ORDER OF DIFFICULTY BY GROUP

Rank (1=most difficult)	Mixed boys	Segregated boys	Mixed girls	Segregated girls
1	Trig problems	Trig problems	Trig problems	Trig problems
2	Using formulas	Using formulas	Using formulas	Problems about scale
3	Solving equations in algebra	Solving equations in algebra	Problems about scale	Geometrical construction
4	Multiplying or dividing fractions	Sets and Venn diagrams	Solving equations in algebra	Reflections or rotations
5	Sets and Venn diagrams	Multiplying or dividing fractions	Reflections or rotations	Using formulas
6	Adding or subtracting fractions	Finding volume	Finding volume	Finding volume
7	Reflections or rotations	Problems about scale	Multiplying or dividing fractions	Multiplying or dividing fractions
8	Finding volume	Calculating with percentages	Adding or subtracting fractions	Multiplying or dividing decimals
9	Problems about scale	Adding or subtracting fractions	Geometrical construction	Using negative numbers
10	Calculating with percentages	Reflections or rotations	Sets and Venn diagrams	Adding or subtracting fractions
11	Averages	Geometrical construction	Calculating with percentages	Adding or subtracting decimals
12	Multiplying or dividing decimals	Using negative numbers	Using negative numbers	Sets and Venn diagrams
13	Number patterns	Averages	Estimating lengths	Calculating with percentages
14	Geometrical construction	Multiplying or dividing decimals	Measuring angles	Solving equations in algebra
15	Adding or subtracting decimals	Everday problems	Averages	Measuring angles

(c) UTILITY SCALE (RANGE 10–50). DISTRIBUTION OF SCORES BY GROUP

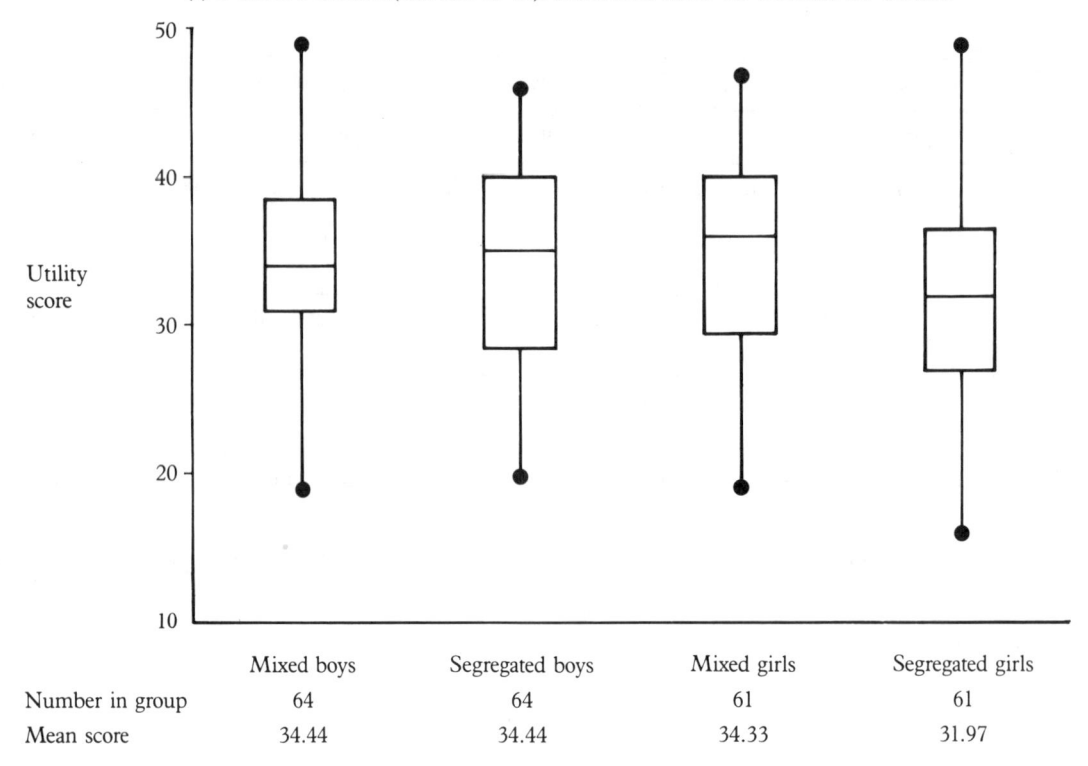

Utility score

	Mixed boys	Segregated boys	Mixed girls	Segregated girls
Number in group	64	64	61	61
Mean score	34.44	34.44	34.33	31.97

(d) ENJOYMENT SCALE (RANGE 7–35). DISTRIBUTION OF SCORES BY GROUP

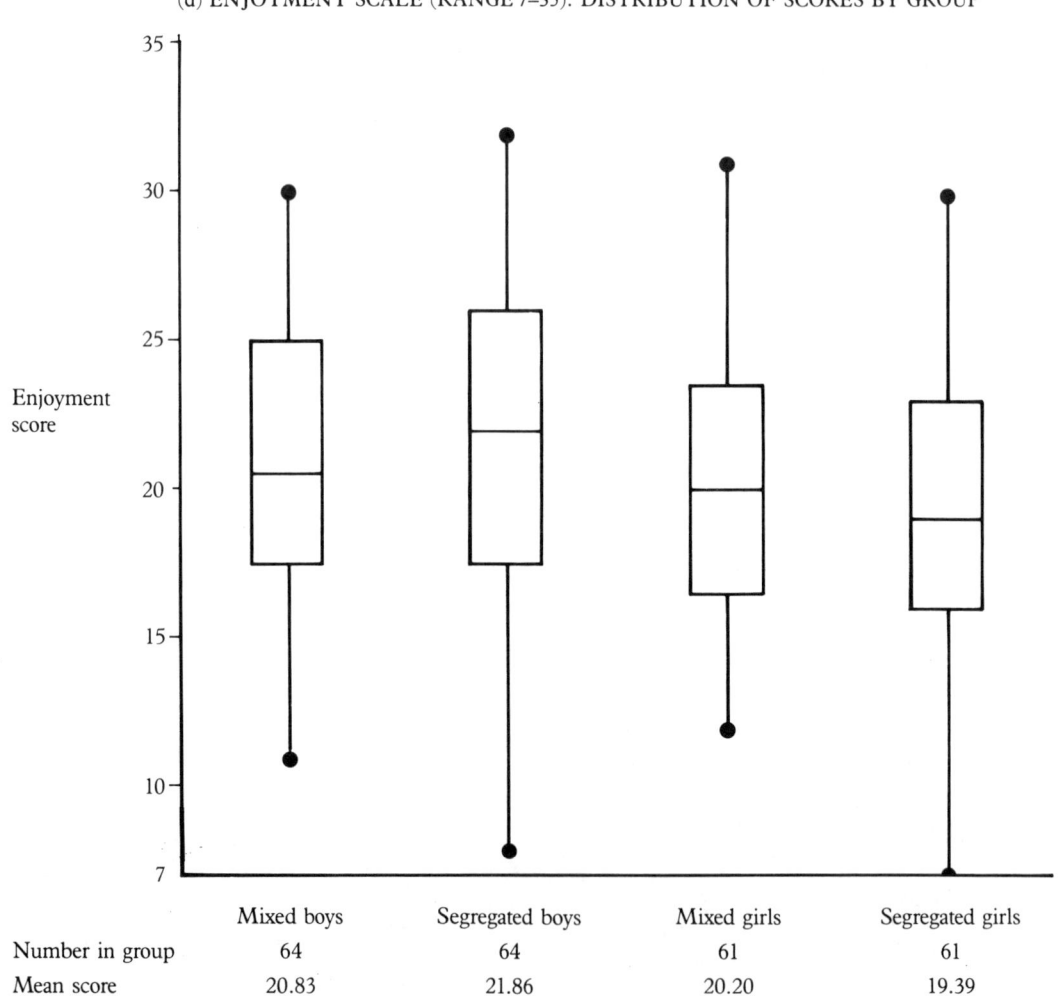

Enjoyment score

	Mixed boys	Segregated boys	Mixed girls	Segregated girls
Number in group	64	64	61	61
Mean score	20.83	21.86	20.20	19.39

References

Assessment of Performance Unit, *Mathematical Development, Primary Survey Report No. 1*, HMSO, 1980.

Assessment of Performance Unit, *Mathematical Development, Primary Survey Report No. 2*, HMSO, 1981.

Assessment of Performance Unit, *Mathematical Development, Secondary Survey Report No. 1*, HMSO, 1980.

Assessment of Performance Unit, *Mathematical Development, Secondary Survey Report No. 2*, HMSO, 1981.

Assessment of Performance Unit, *Mathematical Development, Secondary Survey Report No. 3*, HMSO, 1982.

A. Bone, *Girls and Girls-Only Schools: A Review of the Evidence*, Equal Opportunities Commission, 1983.

G.E.R. Burroughs, *Design and Analysis in Educational Research*, Educational Monograph No. 8, University of Birmingham Faculty of Education, 1971.

A.E. Cameron, 'A comparative study of the mathematical abilities of boys and girls in secondary schools;, M.A. thesis, London, 1923.

W.H. Cockcroft, *Mathematics Counts*, HMSO, 1982.

R.R. Dale, *Mixed or Single Sex School? Vol. III: Attainment, Attitudes and Overview*, Routledge and Kegan Paul, 1974.

Equal Opportunities Commission, *Women and Men in Britain: A Statistical Profile*, 1985.

E. Fennema, 'Mathematics learning and the sexes: a review', *Journal of Research in Mathematics Education*, 5, 1974.

R. Field, 'An inquiry into the relative achievement of boys and girls at a first S.C. examination', M.A. thesis, Birmingham, 1935.

J.P. Guilford, and B. Fruchter, *Fundamental Statistics in Psychology and Education*, McGraw–Hill International, 1981.

Inner London Education Authority, *Sex Differences and Achievement*, RS 823/82, 1982.

W.H. King, 'Comparative attainment in mathematics in single-sex and co-educational secondary schools', *Educational Research*, 8, 2, 1966.

National Foundation for Educational Research, *Achievement in Mathematics*, D.A. Pidgeon, (ed.), 1967.

H.B. Shuard, 'Differences in Mathematical performance between girls and boys', in W.H. Cockcroft, *Mathematics Counts*, HMSO, 1982.

S. Siegel, *Nonparametric Statistics for the Behavioral Sciences*, McGraw–Hill, 1956.

S. Smith, 'Should they be kept apart?' *Times Educational Supplement*, 18th July, 1980.

S. Smith, 'Single-sex Setting', in R. Deem (ed.) *Co-education Reconsidered*, Open University Press, 1984.

J. Steedman, *Progress in Secondary Schools: Findings from the National Child Development Study*, National Childrens Bureau, 1980.

J. Steedman and K. Fogelman, '*Secondary schooling: Findings from the NCDS*', National Childrens Bureau, 1980.

J. Steedman, *Examination Results in Mixed and Single Sex Schools: Findings from the National Child Development Study*, Equal Opportunities Commission, 1983.

M. Sutherland, 'Co-education and school attainment', *British Journal of Educational Psychology*, 31, 2, 1961.

G. Tyson, 'Some apparent effects of co-education suggested by a statistical investigation of examination results', MEd thesis, Manchester, 1928.

R. Walden and V. Walkerdine, *Girls and mathematics: from primary to secondary schooling*, Bedford Way Papers 24, Institute of Education, London University, 1985.

M. Ward, *Mathematics and the 10 year old*, Schools Council Working Paper 61, Evans/Methuen Educational, 1979.

R. Wood and C. Ferguson, 'Unproved case for co-education', *Times Educational Supplement*, 4th October 1974.

R. Wood, 'Sex differences in mathematics attainment at GCE Ordinary Level', *Educational Studies 2*, 2, 1976.